W9-AOB-693

LIBRARY OF LATIN AMERICAN
HISTORY AND CULTURE
GENERAL EDITOR:
DR. A. CURTIS WILGUS

THE EVOLUTION OF

MODERN
LATIN AMERICA

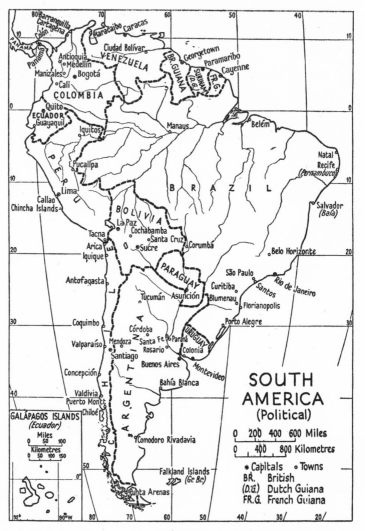

MAP I

THE EVOLUTION OF
MODERN
LATIN AMERICA

BY

ROBIN A. HUMPHREYS

New York
COOPER SQUARE PUBLISHERS, INC.
1973

HOUSTON PUBLIC LIBRARY

R0127007895
sscca

HOUSTON PUBLIC LIBRARY

Originally Published 1946 by Oxford University Press
Reprinted by permission of Oxford University Press
Published 1973 by Cooper Square Publishers, Inc.
59 Fourth Avenue, New York, New York 10003
International Standard Book Number 0-8154-0457-3-
Library of Congress Catalog Card Number 72-94054

Printed in the United States of America

PREFACE

THIS book, which originated in a series of lectures given at Cambridge in the spring of 1945, is designed as an introduction to the modern history of Latin America. It is not primarily a work of research, and its indebtedness to the work of others is everywhere apparent. Its purpose is to examine afresh the evolution of the Latin American states since the achievement of their independence, in the light of changing political, social, and economic conditions, and to interest the student of politics and history in that evolution. The footnotes, and the brief Note on Sources, are intended to serve as a guide to further reading.

It is pleasant to record my obligations to the many friends to whose kindness I owe much, and particularly to Miss Elisabeth Pares, Miss Margaret Goldsmith, Professor David Mitrany, Professor A. G. B. Fisher, and Professor H. Hale Bellot. I am most grateful also to Dr. Brian Roberts, who has designed most of the maps which illustrate the text. To Professor W. L. Burn and to Miss Katharine Duff I owe a special debt, for without their help I doubt whether this book would have been written at all.

R. A. H.

October 1945

CONTENTS

LIST OF MAPS

I

THE SETTING AND THE PEOPLE

FROM the Rio Grande to Cape Horn the twenty
republics of Latin America occupy an area[1] larger by
far than Europe and the United States combined. Brazil,
the colossus of South America, is surpassed among the
nations of the world only by the U.S.S.R., China, and
Canada in territorial extent. Argentina, which competes
with Brazil for leadership in South America, is five times
the size of France. Peru, small in comparison with these
great states, could comfortably contain the whole of the
Union of South Africa; and even the small republics of
Central America, which join the great cornucopia of
Mexico to the vast southern continent, are together equal
in area to Portugal and Spain. Haiti, the smallest of the
Latin American states, is not much larger than Wales.
Brazil, the greatest, is larger than the United States and
almost as large as Europe.

The twenty republics, thus differing in size, differ also
in wealth, culture, race, and population, and they are in
different stages of political, economic, and social evolution.
Except in Portuguese-speaking Brazil and French-speaking
Haiti, they share a common language, the language of the
mother country, Spain. Old lands but new nations, they
have received a similar European inheritance, profoundly
modified in an American environment. They have passed
through a similar colonial experience, and in South America
at least, except for Brazil, they won their independence
by joint endeavour. There are elements of likeness between them also in social structure and political life, and,

---

[1] Roughly 8,000,000 square miles.

B

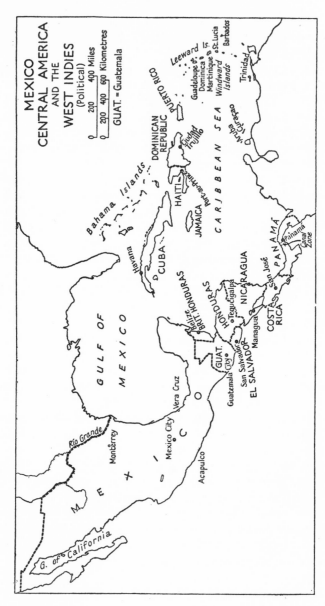

MEXICO
CENTRAL AMERICA
AND THE
WEST INDIES
(Political)

GUAT. = Guatemala

0   200   400   Miles
0 200 400 600 Kilometres

Leeward Is.
Guadeloupe &
Dominica
Martinique
Windward
Islands
•St. Lucia
Barbados

PUERTO RICO

DOMINICAN
REPUBLIC
Ciudad
Trujillo

Trinidad

Bahama Islands

HAITI
Port-au-Prince

CUBA

JAMAICA

CARIBBEAN SEA

Aruba
Curaçao

Havana

GULF OF
MEXICO

Belize
BRIT. HONDURAS

HONDURAS
Tegucigalpa

NICARAGUA

PANAMÁ
Panama
Canal
Zone

GUAT.
Guatemala City•
San Salvador•
EL SALVADOR
Managua•

COSTA
RICA
San José

M   E   X   I   C   O

Mexico City
Vera Cruz

Acapulco

Rio Grande
Montèrrey

G. of California

MAP 2

economically, all are still mainly dependent for their prosperity on the export of a few staple products.

But while, for these reasons, the Latin American republics retain a certain community of sentiments, aspirations, and interests, in each the sense of nationalism is increasingly strong. There are no Latin Americans, except in the sense that a Frenchman and an Austrian are both Europeans; and the relations between the Latin American states themselves, never close, have been marked as much by conflict as by community of interest. Geography and history have been as much dividing as uniting forces in their affairs. The immense size of the Latin American area, its extraordinary physical diversity, and the poverty and sparsity of its peoples have alike tended to isolate from each other the republics which compose it; and though their geographical isolation is now less acute, their historical development has accentuated the great differences and disparities between them.

The republics of the Caribbean area, of course, are closely linked to the United States by proximity and trade as well as policy and strategy. But South America projects far into the southern seas; its southern shores are remote from the great trade-routes of the world; and but 700 miles of icy waters separate it from the great Antarctic continent itself. It lies almost wholly to the east of the United States. On its Pacific coast Valparaíso, the chief port of Chile, which was, until the opening of the Panamá Canal, one of the most inaccessible countries of the world, is east not west of New York. On its Atlantic coast the famous 'bulge' of Brazil is less than 2,000 miles from the shores of Africa. This is the strategic route which unites the Old and the New Worlds across the Atlantic 'narrows'; and because of this easterly extension Buenos Aires and Rio de Janeiro are by sea nearer to Lisbon than to New York.

Only one of the republics, Uruguay, lies wholly outside the tropics or sub-tropical regions. But even in tropical South America, or large parts of it, the effects of altitude counterbalance those of latitude. Half the capital cities of Latin America are situated at heights which vary from just under 2,000 to just under 12,000 feet,[1] and the southern continent is rimmed and deeply penetrated with mountains. On its east coast the great plateau of Brazil and the highlands of Guiana stand steeply from the Atlantic shores. On its west coast the walls of the Andes, rising to formidable heights, stretch from Tierra del Fuego to the Caribbean Sea. They confine Chile to a narrow coastal strip, nearly 3,000 miles long, but rarely more than 100 miles wide. At their greatest width, in central Bolivia, they raise the great plateau, on which the bulk of the Bolivian people dwell, to an average height of two miles above the sea, and imprison it between their western and their eastern cordilleras. In southern Peru these two great chains converge, again divide, march through Ecuador in a majestic avenue of volcanoes, and split in Colombia into three ranges, of which the easternmost sweeps along the Caribbean shores in a double coastal arch. Along the Pacific coast a smaller range links the Andes to the mountain chain of Central America.

Throughout these Andean countries the contrasts of climate and topography are sudden and extravagant. These are the conditions which have made for isolationism and regionalism, for social stratification, and for economic stagnation, and, combined with the poverty of governments, have effectually prevented the full development of the national territories. The eastern valleys of Bolivia, Peru, and Ecuador are, in Isaiah Bowman's words, 'a

---

[1] La Paz, the chief city and actual seat of government of Bolivia, stands at 11,900 feet and is the highest capital city in the world.

paradise', from the point of view both of climate and productivity.[1] But, secluded from the rest of the world by 'mountain barriers on the one side and by distance from ocean ports on the other', as yet they scarcely deserve to be classed among the pioneer lands of the earth.[2] Markets are remote and inaccessible. Settlements are lonely outposts, where life exacts from the European a painful process of adaptation and places the burden of labour upon the backs of natives. Two thousand miles up the Amazon Peru has her Atlantic port at Iquitos, and to travel from Lima to Iquitos takes four hours by air. But so arduous was the land route and so formidable the mountain barrier, that until the opening of the great Lima–Tingo María–Pucallpa highway that serves to link these towns together by road and river, travellers might well prefer to make the journey by way of the Panamá Canal, Brazil, and the Amazon itself.

In the lowlands nature is equally exuberant and its effects are equally impressive. Between the coastal arch of northern Venezuela and the highlands of Guiana lie the *llanos*, one of the three great plains regions of South America, stretching from the Atlantic to the Colombian Andes and alternately drained and drenched by the waters of the Orinoco. It was up this stream, or rather flood, that Ralegh sought El Dorado and the 'Large, Rich and Bewtiful Empyre of Guiana'. From here Bolívar launched his great campaign for the liberation of New Granada, and it is in the highlands to the south that Hudson's 'Green Mansions' lie. These plains are cattle country, but even for cattle they are ill adapted, and for the white man they have offered less a livelihood than a grave.

[1] Isaiah Bowman, ed., *Limits of Land Settlement* (New York, Council on Foreign Relations, 1937), p. 299.

[2] R. R. Platt, in *Pioneer Settlement. Coöperative Studies by Twenty-Six Authors* (New York, American Geographical Society, 1932), pp. 98 and 107.

THE
SURFACE FEATURES
OF
SOUTH AMERICA

0   200   400   600 Miles
0   200 400 600 800 Kilometres

High Mountains (Over 15,000 ft.)
Rugged Mountains (5,000-15,000 ft.)
Plateaus and Uplands (500-5,000 ft.)
Lowlands and Plains (0-500 ft.)

MAP 3

Farther south again, and confined between the Andes, the highlands of Guiana, and the great plateau of Brazil, lies the vast inland world of Amazonia, the second and greatest of the great plains regions of South America, embracing an area as large as that of all of the United States between the Atlantic and the Mississippi, and barely separated from the Orinoco plains on the one hand (the waters of the Amazon and the waters of the Orinoco are in fact connected) and from the headwaters of the Paraguay and the Río de la Plata system on the other.[1] Settlement in these Amazon lowlands is not impracticable. The rubber boom early in this century brought prosperity and an opera-house to Manaus. But, to quote Isaiah Bowman again, 'to the white man a tropical settlement is still like the medieval walled town: the wild beasts of legend are the microbes, and the wall is medical science. It still costs too much to keep the wall in repair, and commercial development is aimed primarily at money making, not the conquest of tropical diseases.'[2] The Amazon basin must long remain a world of its own, a world in which the European can barely maintain the struggle for existence against climate and disease.

The intensive efforts made of late years to exploit the rubber resources of the Amazon valley as a substitute for Far Eastern sources of supply do not reverse this judgement. But there are great areas which border the Amazon basin empty of people and suitable for settlement. The highlands of Mato Grosso, far to the interior of Brazil, constitute one

[1] W. L. Schurz, *Latin America* (New York, Dutton, 1942), p. 26, points out that at a certain season of the year it would be possible to travel by water from the mouth of the Orinoco to the mouth of the Río de la Plata without entering the Atlantic and with only a short portage at the divide between the Amazon and Paraguay systems.

[2] Isaiah Bowman, *The Pioneer Fringe* (New York, American Geographical Society, 1931), p. 56.

of the largest tracts of undeveloped country in the world,[1] though they offer only the hardest forms of pioneer life; and to the development of this area the Central Brazilian Foundation, established in 1943, has been directing its attention. The open plains at the foot of the Bolivian Andes, near Santa Cruz de la Sierra, are a similar area whose development is retarded by a similar inaccessibility. Their colonization can only be undertaken by large-scale methods. But Argentina and Brazil each hope by road and rail to tap the rich resources of this fertile hinterland.

The third of the great plains regions of South America is the Argentine pampa, bordered to the south by the bare and wind-swept plateaux of Patagonia, to the west by an arid and mountainous Andean region, and to the north by sub-tropical lands. It extends from the sea to the Andes about 700 miles. 'Over all this immense space', wrote an early traveller, 'there is not a tree, not a shrub, nor a single perennial plant to be seen, save only those few which here and there lift their heads near a herdsman's hut. There are no hills nor eminences, and the undulations are so gentle as only to be perceived by taking a long view over its surface.'[2] This was the land of the Argentine cow-boy, the gaucho, so vividly portrayed in the pages of Sarmiento; and on its immense productivity in cattle, sheep, and corn the prosperity of modern Argentina is built.

No road joins the southern to the northern continent. For four centuries the passage across the isthmus of Panamá has been one of the great trade-routes of the world. As early as 1529 the project of a Panamá Canal was born. But the isthmus is a barrier, not a link between the con-

---

[1] See W. L. Schurz, 'Conditions affecting Settlement on the Matto Grosso Highland and in the Gran Chaco', in *Pioneer Settlement*, pp. 108–23.

[2] W. R. Manning, ed., *Diplomatic Correspondence of the United States concerning the Independence of the Latin-American Nations* (3 vols., New York, Carnegie Endowment, 1925), i. 400.

tinents. Jungle and swamp form a still impenetrable frontier between Colombia and Panamá. Even Tschiffely, on his famous ride from Buenos Aires to New York, did this stretch by sea. Middle America, as it is convenient to term this region between Panamá and the Rio Grande, repeats a familiar pattern of coastal plain, mountain, and plateau. The small republics of Central America itself dwell in a state of mutual attraction and repulsion, and for them Mexico, the third in size of the Latin American countries, the second in population, and the only one contiguous to the United States, is the 'colossus of the north'. Here also the contrasts of climate and topography are sudden and astonishing. The great central Mexican table-land is flanked by towering mountain ranges, whose irregular heights rise to 18,000 feet, and the traveller who follows the route of Cortés from the port of Vera Cruz climbs within a few hours from the tropical heat of the *tierra caliente* to the chill of the *tierra fría*, more than 6,000 feet up, before arriving at Mexico City itself and its crowning glories of Popocatépetl and Ixtaccihuatl.

The sea has been the traditional link between the Latin American republics. The land divides; the sea unites. Only Bolivia and Paraguay are completely landlocked, and even Paraguay has access to the sea by the Paraguay and Paraná. But the Latin American countries have possessed no extensive mercantile marines, and even by sea communications are difficult. On the west coast, between the Andes and the Pacific and between Colombia and Chile, perpetual rain gradually gives place to perpetual drought, forest and swamp to the desert fringe of the Peruvian shores; while from southern Peru to Coquimbo in Chile stretches a rainless, treeless plain, rich only in nitrates and copper. Mists overhang the land, and the south and south-westerly winds pile high the Pacific rollers. Even in central

Chile the great port of Valparaíso is not immune from damage by the sea. In southern Chile the coastline is extremely broken and abounds in labyrinthine turnings. But this southern region, drenched by summer rains and winter snows, is almost as inhospitable as the desert north. Nor is the Atlantic coast of Patagonia much more favourable. Winds sweep over it, and storms, tides, and mud choke its harbours. The port of Bahía Blanca, like that of Buenos Aires itself, requires perpetual dredging. Uruguay and Brazil are more favoured by nature. But Venezuela and the Caribbean shores of Colombia are washed by shallow seas, and only small boats may approach their ports and harbours.

Four river systems—the Magdalena, the Orinoco, the Amazon, and the La Plata basin—drain the southern continent. But they have not joined the peoples. The Amazon is indeed navigable for ocean-going ships 2,000 miles up. Corumbá, high on the Paraguay, is a remote Brazilian port for small river-craft from Buenos Aires, 1,400 miles away. But the navigation of the Paraguay and Paraná is costly and difficult. Tributaries of the Amazon drain the lowlands of eastern Bolivia. But the rivers change their course; floods sweep over them; rapids obstruct them; their banks crumble and decay; trees and tropical growth block their channels. In southern Brazil the rivers flow, not from the interior to the Atlantic coast, but from the great Atlantic escarpment to the interior. Even the historic São Francisco, which has played so great a part in the evolution of Brazil, and may yet play a greater, flows for a thousand miles to the north before it turns to plunge over one of the world's great waterfalls on its way to the sea.

It is outwards across the oceans rather than inwards across the land that the natural routes of communication and the economic interests of the Latin American states

have lain. The rapid and spectacular growth of air transport has now brought Buenos Aires within seven hours,
instead of six days, of Rio de Janeiro, and Bogotá within
three hours, instead of eight days, of Barranquilla, at the
mouth of the Magdalena. In Central America and southern
Patagonia cattle or sheep take wing and chickens fly to
market. The aeroplane has begun to supersede the railway,
the road, and the trail in the pattern of everyday living.
This is a revolution, one of many revolutions now taking
place in Latin America. But vast areas of the continent
still remain dependent on the cart-track and the mule-
trail; and just as a large proportion of the agricultural
population of Latin America has lived and still lives in
conditions hardly more civilized than at the time of the
conquest, so, within the interior, communications are
equally primitive. Buenos Aires, São Paulo, and Rio de
Janeiro each have their railway networks. Chile has its
famous longitudinal line. There are railways in Bolivia,
Peru, and Ecuador, as well as in Brazil, which are miracles
of technical skill. But ten years ago, less than a fifth of
South America lay within twenty miles of a railway.[1] Nor
by road were communications much easier. The great
Pan American highway, which is to link New York to
Buenos Aires, will have a political as well as an economic
justification. But the difficulties of its construction are
themselves a measure of the isolation in which the republics
of the New World have lived one from another.

Within the whole of Latin America there are fewer people
than in the United States.[2] Brazil contains nearly half the
population of the southern continent and could, under
favourable conditions, support some 400 millions or more

[1] Bowman, *The Pioneer Fringe*, p. 305.
[2] Under 130,000,000, including European possessions in the Latin
American area.

MAP 4

The Railways of Latin America, 1944

of people. Yet Brazil, which is larger than the United States, has a smaller population than the British Isles. The average density is under 13 to the square mile.[1] Haiti, with 252 persons to the square mile, and El Salvador, with 136, are the most densely peopled of the Latin American countries. They are also the smallest. Of the rest, only three, Guatemala, Cuba, and the Dominican Republic, have a population density of more than 50 to the square mile, and, except for Uruguay, Mexico, Costa Rica, and Nicaragua, the figure is under 25.

Even these figures, small as they are, are misleading, for the population of the Latin American countries is not evenly distributed either between or within the several states. It follows a grouped or clustered pattern, and the population clusters on the coast, and in the interior, are, for the most part, separated by great distances or sparsely peopled territories. The coast of Brazil, for example, resembles an archipelago, a group of inhabited islands, rather than a continuous area of settlement. Only rarely do these scattered groups spread out widely, and there are, on the mainland of Latin America, few zones of concentrated rural settlement.[2] To an extraordinary degree, indeed, the pattern of settlement established in colonial days still survives. The movement of conquest and colonization carried the Spaniards from north to south and west to east of South America with giant strides and almost incredible rapidity, and already by the end of the sixteenth century most of

[1] England and Wales (1940), 703; United States, 44·2; Australia, 2·2.
[2] Preston E. James, *Latin America* (London, Cassell, 1943), p. 4, lists as examples of such areas the central zone of Mexico; the highlands of Guatemala and El Salvador; the intermont basins of Costa Rica; the Antioquia region of Colombia; possibly some of the high basins of the Peruvian Andes and certainly a part of the borders of Lake Titicaca; the Cochabamba basin of Bolivia; parts of northern middle Chile; the oasis of Tucumán in Argentina; and parts of the north-east coast of Brazil.

MAP 5

The Roads of Latin America, 1944

what are to-day the chief cities of Spanish America dotted the map like Roman *coloniae*, centres of civilization in the wilderness. But isolated centres they long remained. In North America the English colonies in the seventeenth century were a pioneer fringe on the Atlantic coast. The land beyond the Alleghany mountains was an unknown land. But the scattered settlements grew together. The frontier zone moved from tide-water to up-country. It climbed the mountain ridges, and in the nineteenth century the relentless movement of western expansion carried the settled area from the Alleghanies to the Pacific.

In Latin America there has been no 'moving frontier' strictly comparable to the great movement of western expansion in the United States. The conquest of the northern and the conquest of the southern continent followed different lines. There have been frontier movements in Latin America, and throughout the continent the frontier, as a zone between civilization and the wilderness, is a political, an economic, and a social fact. But the expanding frontiers of Latin America were, in the main, 'hollow frontiers'.[1] They rolled forward as waves of exploitation and they left behind a depopulated, sometimes a devastated, area. Only rarely, as in the peopling of southern Brazil and south-central Chile, have they been true frontiers of expanding settlement.[2]

The result is to be seen on any population map. The towns have drained the country. Rural and urban expansion have failed to grow together. Vast areas of the continent are almost uninhabited. Even in Argentina the characteristic feature is the concentration of people in

[1] James, op. cit., pp. 5–6.
[2] Professor James notes four zones of expanding settlement at present— the highlands of Costa Rica, the highlands of Antioquia, the Central Valley of Chile, and the three southern states of Brazil. (Loc. cit.)

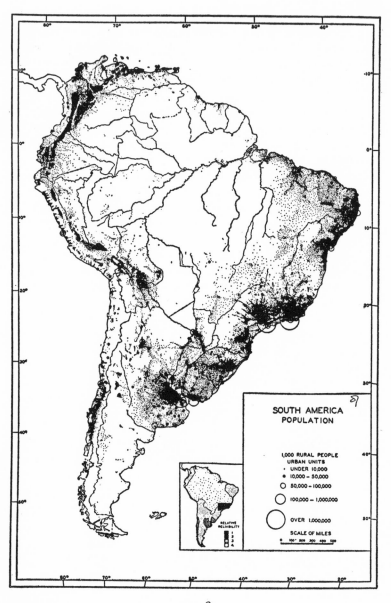

SOUTH AMERICA
POPULATION

1,000 RURAL PEOPLE
URBAN UNITS
· UNDER 10,000
• 10,000 – 50,000
○ 50,000 – 100,000
◯ 100,000 – 1,000,000
◯ OVER 1,000,000

SCALE OF MILES
0 100 200 300 400 500

RELATIVE
RELIABILITY
1
2
3
4

MAP 6

Buenos Aires and its hinterland. More than a third of Argentina's fourteen millions of people live in Buenos Aires and the Province of Buenos Aires. In Brazil five states, Minas Gerais, São Paulo, Baía, Pernambuco, and Rio Grande do Sul, account for more than a half of the total population and only a fifth of the total area. The two key states, Minas Gerais and São Paulo, alone contain more than a third. In Chile the fertile central valley is the favoured region, and in Bolivia the bleak highlands, which constitute only a fifth part of the total area of the country, contain three-quarters of the population. Peru, Colombia, and Venezuela repeat the same pattern. Only two of the mainland republics, El Salvador and Uruguay, Professor Preston James believes, make effective use of all parts of their national territories,[1] and it is doubtful whether even this is not an over-estimate rather than an under-estimate.

The racial composition of this population is extremely varied. This also is strongly reflected in the political and economic life of the republics. At the end of the colonial period there were, according to the estimates of Humboldt,[2] some seventeen millions of people in Spanish America. Of these, three and a quarter millions were white and seven and a half were Indian. The remainder, except for three-quarters of a million negroes, were mestizo, the product of the mingling of the blood of the conquerors with the blood of the conquered. There were, perhaps, nearly another two million negroes, out of a total population of some four or five millions, in the old Portuguese colony of Brazil.[3]

[1] James, op. cit., p. 4.
[2] Alexander von Humboldt, *Personal Narrative of Travels to the Equinoctial Regions of the New Continent, during the years 1799–1804* (trans. Helen Maria Williams, 7 vols., London, 1814–29), vi. 127, 836.
[3] For the population of Brazil in the eighteen-twenties see J. F. Normano, *Brazil, a Study of Economic Types* (Chapel Hill, Univ. of North Carolina Press, 1935), p. 81.

4921   C

These were the descendants of slaves or themselves the victims of the slave-trade.

To-day, after a further century of population growth, of European and Asiatic immigration, and of intermarriage, there are only three countries, Argentina, Uruguay, and Costa Rica, whose population is almost wholly white—countries, that is, in which the white population constitutes more than four-fifths of the whole. In Costa Rica, that small oasis of democracy amidst a desert of Central American dictators, the Indian stock, never large, had been reduced to negligible proportions already by the end of the colonial period.[1] In Argentina, where, more than in any other Latin American country, the white population has been swelled by immigration, pioneers and Indians, as in the United States, were hereditary enemies. The first Spanish settlement at Buenos Aires, like the first English settlement at Jamestown in Virginia, fell before the fury of Indian attack. But as in the United States, so in Argentina, the nomadic Indians of the plains were ruthlessly extruded or exterminated. Their final subjugation by General Roca in the campaigns of the seventies and eighties was only a repetition of the tragic history of pioneer advance in North America. What the sword and the musket have failed to do, disease has now nearly accomplished.

In Chile the reverse process has taken place, and in Chile the white and Indian elements have been almost completely fused. Not till the eighteen-sixties and seventies were the fierce Araucanians, immortalized in the great epic of Alonso de Ercilla y Zúñiga, finally subdued and tranquillized and their last refuge in the deep forests south of the Bío-Bío and north of Valdivia opened to colonization. There are few

[1] See C. L. Jones, *Costa Rica and Civilisation in the Caribbean* (Madison, Univ. of Wisconsin Studies in the Social Sciences and History, No. 23, 1935), p. 35.

pure-blooded Indians left in Chile, but the Indians have been absorbed rather than exterminated. From the founding of Santiago by Pedro de Valdivia in the sixteenth century, Spanish civilization in Chile has been engrafted. on to Indian stock. Landowner and peasant, master and man, are sharply divided by wealth, education, status, power; but they boast the same mingling of Spanish and Araucanian blood. Though the peasantry are more directly descended from the Indians and the upper classes are more nearly European in extraction, they belong to the same new and distinctively Chilean race.[1]

No such complete amalgamation has yet taken place in Brazil; but Brazil, even more than the United States, is the 'melting-pot' of America. The basic element of the population is white, notably increased by European immigration, Latin and non-Latin, in the late nineteenth and early twentieth centuries. The minor strains are negro and Indian. There is probably less racial prejudice in Brazil than in any country in the world, and from the mingling of these stocks there has sprung a remarkable variety of types and colours, united by the fact that they are all Brazilian. Half the population may, by courtesy, be classified as white, but there is a high proportion composed of mulattoes, zambos, and mestizos, particularly mulattoes, and there is a strong admixture also of pure negroes. Brazil, like the United States, was a slave-holding state. The traffic in men began early in the sixteenth century. It was not abolished till 1850 nor completely suppressed till 1852, while the 'peculiar institution' of slavery itself survived till 1888, when the emancipation of the slaves, without compensation to

[1] G. M. McBride, *Chile: Land and Society* (New York, American Geographical Society, 1936), p. 13. A similar amalgamation has taken place in Paraguay, though here the Indian is the predominant strain. Paraguay is the only country in which an Indian language (Guaraní) is employed in important newspapers and also, from time to time, in official speeches.

their owners, was one of the causes of the collapse of the Brazilian Empire. Like the United States also, Brazil has its broad division between north and south. But in Brazil it is the southern states, of São Paulo, Paraná, Santa Catarina, and Rio Grande do Sul, that are predominantly peopled by whites. The negroes are most numerous in the coastal regions of the central and northern parts of the country, and above all in Baía. 'We never go very far into a person's past', a Baían remarked. 'That would be impolite.' But even in Baía, which so long served as one of the four great ports of entry for negro slaves, both 'pure' whites and 'pure' negroes are relatively few.[1] The absorption of the negro is in Brazil not merely a matter of national policy but of social and biological fact. There is no race problem in Brazil as that problem is known in the United States. Class not race is the determinant of status.

The Indian element is relatively less important. In São Paulo there is now little trace of that cross-breeding which produced the *mamelucos*, the famous *bandeirantes*, who, in search of gold and Indians to enslave, performed phenomenal feats of exploration and carried the frontiers of Brazil far into the interior. But the evidences of cross-breeding are still strong in the northern and north-eastern states, and in the forests of the Amazon or on the interior plateaux the Indian tribes still live much in their primitive state. No one yet has ventured with safety into the territory of the fierce Chavantes of central Brazil, who shoot even at aeroplanes with their bows and arrows; and the Brazilian Government in general follows a policy which leaves the savage Indians undisturbed but affords a degree of protection to the civilized Indians through the 'Serviço de

[1] Donald Pierson, *Negroes in Brazil. A Study of Race Contact at Bahia* (Univ. of Chicago Press, 1942), pp. 36, 128, and 131.

Proteção aos Indios', headed by the celebrated General Rondón, himself a full-blooded Indian.

Four countries, Bolivia, Peru, Ecuador, and Guatemala, are predominantly Indian countries, though in each a small white, or—for the term is elastic—*soi-disant* white and mestizo minority holds the reins of political and economic power. Mexico, Colombia, Venezuela, Paraguay, and most of the Central American countries are Indian and mestizo. The Indians, whose ancestors, in remote time, crossed the Bering Straits and penetrated from North to South America (the theory that the Incas of Peru were Japanese may be classed with the view that the American Indians are really Welsh) represent varied stocks and linguistic groups. Even in modern Mexico some fifty Indian languages are spoken. But there is a broad distinction between the primitive tribes of the tropical forests, the hunters of the plains, and the sedentary Indians of the mountain ranges. These, from Bolivia to Colombia and northern Central America to Mexico, are the fallen heirs of the relatively advanced cultures of pre-conquest times, of the Incas, the Chibchas, the Mayas, the Aztecs.

But they are much fallen. Where the native populations were densest, there the seats of Spanish power were strongest. In the anxiety to defend Spain against the charges of cruelty and tyranny so freely levelled against her from the days of Bartolomé de las Casas, the Apostle of the Indians, onwards, there is a danger of replacing the *leyenda negra* by a *leyenda blanca*. It is to the credit of Spain as a colonizing Power that if she exploited the Indians she also tried to save their souls. The religious and the acquisitive impulses were equally strong. But whatever the views of the royal and ecclesiastical authorities at home on Spain's imperial mission and the 'white man's burden', in the colonies the Indians were reduced to serfdom, and serfs they have remained. The state of peonage in which they frequently live in Bolivia, in the interior provinces of Peru and Ecuador, and in other parts of Latin America as well, is little more than a politer name for slavery.[1] In none of the four predominantly Indian countries of Latin America is much more than a quarter of the population able to read or write, and in some the proportion is less. The Indian, so far as he is assimilated into society at all, remains on its lowest fringe, valued merely as a source of labour for the plantations, the ranches, and the mines. Divided from the past, ill adapted to the present, impoverished, often degenerate, diseased, or sunk in a hopeless apathy, and governed by a social, cultural, and economic pattern fundamentally different from that of the European, the Indians, at least in Peru or Bolivia, are in, but not of, the nation. The incorporation of these native stocks into the national life is one of the fundamental problems which the Indian countries of Latin America still face in their long struggle to attain to national unity and social coherence.

The Indian has been the forgotten man of Latin America. He is now being rediscovered. The archaeologists and anthropologists are in part responsible for this.[2] So also is the contemporary spirit of nationalism and an awakening social conscience in some at least of the Indian and mestizo countries. The Mexican revolution, the first genuine social revolution in America, was accompanied by a self-conscious exaltation of the virtues of the Indian, contrasted with the vices of the Spaniards (both exemplified in the frescoes of Rivera and the more cynical art of Orozco) as well as by a

[1] Cf. Bowman, *The Pioneer Fringe*, p. 297, and *The Andes of Southern Peru* (New York, American Geographical Society, 1916), p. 25. See also *Labour Problems in Bolivia. Report of the Joint Bolivian-United States Labour Commission* (Montreal, International Labour Office, 1943), p. 7.

[2] Cf. C. C. Griffin, ed., *Concerning Latin American Culture* (New York, Columbia Univ. Press, 1940), p. 120.

vigorous attempt to improve the Indian's lot and a passion for rural education. In Peru the Alianza Popular Revolucionaria Americana, led by the mild Haya de la Torre, has preferred to think in terms of Indo-America rather than of Spanish or Latin America. This, the most remarkable indigenous political philosophy that Latin America has produced, is a compound of agrarian socialism and Indo-American nationalism. In a country which is highly conservative in religion, oligarchical in politics, and semi-feudal in its organization, Apra has taken for its aim the unification of the peasants, the intellectuals, and the urban workers. It long operated outside the law. Now renamed the Partido del Pueblo, and at last given legal recognition, it still represents perhaps the most important single force in Peruvian politics, and bears distinct resemblances in its programme to that pursued in Mexico since the revolution of 1910.

But the mestizo is the true American man, and the path of the Indian lies along the line of miscegenation. There is little to relieve the gloom in which the Indian's present lot is cast. But there is nothing to prove that the mestizo, given the time and the opportunity, cannot become the equal of the white. Whatever the moral that may be drawn, Colombia, a mestizo and Indian country, is one of the more genuinely democratic of the Latin American states. Mexico, Indian and mestizo, has attacked, and with some measure of success, a task of social regeneration of extraordinary complexity; and the student of Latin American history, confronted with the problems of political disorder and social disunity, will do well to beware of the refuge of racial explanations.

In the three island republics of Latin America, Cuba, the Dominican Republic, and Haiti, the negro strain again becomes important, though negroes, mainly West Indian coloured labourers, are scattered throughout Central

America. They form, for example, a considerable proportion of the population of Panamá, and their arrival, to work on the banana plantations, has caused considerable alarm in Costa Rica and other of the countries of this area. Negroes are also common in the hot coastal regions of Venezuela and Colombia and, to a lesser extent, of Ecuador and Peru. Haiti, however, like Liberia, is a negro republic, whose population is almost wholly descended from the negro slaves of the old French colony of Saint Domingue. Here the tiny ruling mulatto class assiduously cultivates, and sometimes caricatures, the virtues of French civilization. The Dominican Republic, which uneasily shares the island of Santo Domingo with Haiti, in pointed contrast to its 'black' and over-populated neighbour, claims to be 'white'. Its 'pure' negro population is, in point of fact, comparatively small, but so also is its 'pure' white, and the bulk of the population consists of persons of mixed race. Finally, in Cuba, which was, with Puerto Rico, the last part of the Spanish Empire to survive in the New World, the major strains are again European and negro. So early was the native Indian race virtually exterminated that negro slaves were introduced even in 1523 and slavery itself survived till 1886. The population, swelled by a variety of immigrants, is extraordinarily heterogeneous, and the negroes themselves have been more assimilated than in the United States. Their social progress, however, is even less.

This picture of man and his environment in Latin America is not without its dark and forbidding aspects. If New York is not America, still less is Buenos Aires Argentina or Rio de Janeiro Brazil. Yet the civilizations of the Latin American countries are interesting in themselves and they give promise of new and vigorous life. John Quincy Adams, describing the emancipation of this vast area from the dominion of Spain and Portugal at the opening of the last century, declared that it was 'a mighty movement in human affairs, mightier far than that of the downfall of the Roman Empire'.[1] This was exaggeration. Yet the emancipation of Latin America more ·than a century ago was one of the formative events of modern history. It marked a further stage in the shift from a Mediterranean to an Atlantic civilization. It opened a vast area, hitherto closed by the policies of Spain and Portugal, to trade and immigration. It brought into existence a variety of new states, and in politics, in strategy, and in commerce, it was destined to have far-reaching effects on the balance of world affairs.

A hundred years is not a long time in the life of a nation, and few peoples have set out, as the Latin American peoples set out, on a career of independent nationhood with such initial disadvantages. Self-government and democracy are not to be won overnight. But the events of the last half-century have wrought deep changes in the political and economic life of the major republics. Hitherto they have been junior rather than equal partners in the society of nations. They were objects of policy, children at the international table. But not only does the Latin American area constitute one of the richest raw material producing regions of the world; the Latin American states are themselves increasing in wealth and power and in political and economic maturity. Their future development, their stability or instability, their political and economic policies, their problems and prospects, must be increasingly important to the rest of the world. Amidst the revolution in world affairs in which we now live, Latin America has an active political as well as economic importance.

[1] C. K. Webster, *Britain and the Independence of Latin America, 1812–1830: Select Documents from the Foreign Office Archives* (2 vols., Oxford Univ. Press, 1938), i. 3.

II

THE EMANCIPATION OF LATIN AMERICA

SPANISH civilization is deeply imprinted on Spanish America, in the imperial splendour of the great Viceregal capitals of Lima and Mexico City, in churches and palaces, in law and custom, in outward forms and inward life. 'What Rome did for Spain', Edward Gaylord Bourne has remarked, 'Spain in turn did for Spanish America.'[1] Only Portugal rivalled Spain in the extent of her dominions, and though the achievements of Portugal were less spectacular, Brazil is as much Portuguese as Spanish America is Spanish. For three hundred years, moreover, and in the face of bitter colonial rivalries, Spain gave her empire substantial peace. Even at the end of the eighteenth century, when she had abandoned her exclusive claims to the northwest coast of North America and had parted also with the ill-defined area of Louisiana (ceded by Spain to France and sold by Napoleon to the United States), Spain still held sway from California to Cape Horn.

Yet, within twenty-five years, the two islands of Cuba and Puerto Rico were all that remained of this vast empire. In the struggle for North American independence the thirteen English colonies emerged as one United States. But between 1810 and 1830 thirteen states replaced the former empires of Spain and Portugal. The map of the New World was redrawn. In South America the Spanish Viceroyalty of La Plata split, along the lines of old administrative divisions, into the United Provinces of the Río de la Plata (modern Argentina), Paraguay, and Bolivia; and Uruguay was also carved from its territory to act as a buffer state between

[1] *Spain in America, 1450–1580* ('The American Nation', vol. iii, New York and London, Harper, 1904), p. 202.

Argentina and Brazil. On the west coast the republics of
Chile and Peru replaced the former Spanish Captaincy-
General and Viceroyalty respectively. Farther north, the
vast republic of (Great) Colombia, which the liberator,
Bolívar, had created out of the Viceroyalty of New Granada,
dissolved by 1830 into the three states of Ecuador, New
Granada (Colombia), and Venezuela. Brazil, in 1822, by
a singularly peaceful revolution, became an independent
empire, under the House of Bragança, and, an empire amid
republics, so remained till 1889. In North America,
Mexico passed rapidly from viceroyalty to empire and from
empire to republic. What are now the five states of Central
America joined, in 1823, to form the Confederation of the
United Provinces of Central America, which survived only
till 1838; and Haiti, which declared its independence from
France in 1804, extended its rule over the Spanish colony
of Santo Domingo. It was not till 1844, however, that the
Dominican Republic threw off the rule of Haiti, and it was
again incorporated with Spain from 1861 to 1865; and not
till 1902 that Cuba finally attained to self-government, after
the Spanish-American war had swept away the last vestiges
of Spanish empire in the New World. Lastly, it was only in
1903 that Panamá, the youngest of the republics, with the
timely assistance of President Theodore Roosevelt, successfully established its independence of Colombia.

The area affected by the Spanish American wars of independence was far greater than that affected by the war of
North American independence. The peoples involved were
far more numerous; the contest was bloodier; and the
struggle lasted twice as long. To the revolt of the English
colonies in North America both France and Spain lent their
aid. No outside Power came to the formal assistance of the
Spanish American peoples. The loyalists were numerous; a
large section of the people was indifferent, and indifferently

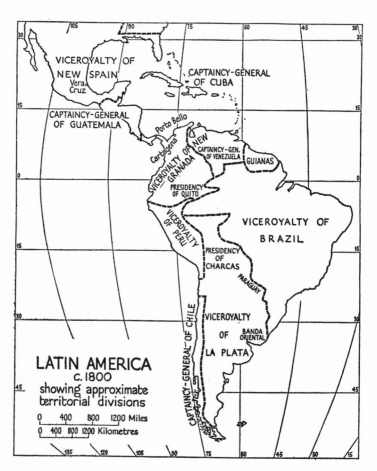

MAP 7

LATIN AMERICA
c. 1826
showing approximate
territorial divisions

0   400   800   1200 Miles

0   400 800 1200 Kilometres

All boundaries are approximate.
Dotted boundaries are still
more vaguely defined

MAP 8

changed sides; and the wars were civil wars, conducted with a Spanish ferocity, and leaving in their train a wake of terrible devastation. To some, perhaps indeed to most, the struggle was unmeaning, save as a relaxation of authority or a change of masters. But like the earlier revolution in North America, the revolutions for Latin American independence were not merely struggles for home-rule, complicated by the division between patriots and loyalists; they were conflicts also over who should rule at home; and while the emancipation of Spanish America involved a political revolution and to some extent also an economic revolution, it stopped short at the point where it might have involved a social revolution. At the end, the structure of colonial society, inherited from medieval Spain, remained essentially unchanged, with the sole exception that the Spaniards born in America now stood in the shoes of the Spaniards born in Spain.

The American Revolution presented the first example of freedom in the New World; and, as Canning rightly held, 'the operation of that example, sooner or later, was inevitable'.[1] The French Revolution presented a similar example from the Old World, and its effects were still more profound. It was not possible to withhold from the more educated or travelled of creoles the knowledge of American—and English—political ideas or French revolutionary thought. Bolívar, the greatest of Latin American statesmen, was himself educated by his tutor according to the best principles of *Émile*; in Buenos Aires Mariano Moreno, 'the soul of the revolutionary movement in Argentina', as Belaunde has described him, reprinted the *Social Contract* in 1810;[2] and

[1] Webster, *Britain and the Independence of Latin America*, i. 6.

[2] It was not the only edition. One appeared in Caracas in 1809 and another in Mexico City in 1822. Cf. J. R. Spell, 'Rousseau in Spanish America', *Hispanic American Historical Review*, xv (1935), pp. 260–7; and V. A. Belaunde, *Bolívar and the Political Thought of the Spanish American Revolu-*

Miranda, the father of Venezuelan independence, was a French revolutionary general as well as much else in the course of his astonishing career. It was, moreover, the French Revolution in its Napoleonic aspect[1] which precipitated both the Spanish American revolutions and that flight of the Portuguese royal family to Brazil which resulted in a sudden and all-important reversal in the respective positions of Brazil and Portugal.

A third outside influence also operated upon the Spanish colonies, in a less obvious but equally decisive way. The wealth of the Indies had always been the envy of Europe. 'It is his [the King of Spain's] Indian gold', wrote Ralegh, 'that endangereth and disturbeth all the nations of Europe.' The Spanish Empire was the world's storehouse of the precious metals. But it was more than a treasure-house; it was a market of unknown potentialities. In vain Spain tried to preserve these resources for herself; her enemies exhausted her first by plunder, then by trade. From the sixteenth century onwards the empire was gradually enmeshed in a net of foreign pressure, which grew steadily stronger after, in the seventeenth century, Spain's rivals found a foothold in the Spanish Main. Finally, the commercial expansion of Europe, and particularly of England, gathering speed at the end of the eighteenth century, enhanced to the Spanish colonists the prospects of expanding markets and increased sources of supply, and heightened the pressure of the Old World (and, indeed, of the infant United States itself) to break the gigantic monopoly which Spain had erected but could not exploit in the New.

tion (Baltimore, Johns Hopkins Press, 1938), pp. 22–37. Note also Miranda's conversations with Samuel Adams. W. S. Robertson, ed., The Diary of Francisco de Miranda (New York, Hispanic Society of America, 1928), p. 118, and for the young Bolívar see Jules Mancini's admirable and entertaining Bolívar et L'Émancipation des Colonies Espagnoles des Origines à 1815 (Paris, Perrin et Cie, 1912). [1] Webster, op. cit., i. 8.

For to a degree unparalleled by her rivals Spain subjected her colonies to a closed monopolistic system and imposed upon them a paternal autocracy. The empire was administered as a centralized absolutism, with elaborate checks and balances designed to prevent maladministration on the part of the servants of the Crown. Power, however benevolently intended, came from above. In the English colonies in North America the colonists were from the first educated to self-government. Experience was their guide when, throwing off the bonds of England, they came to form the Constitution of the United States. The fathers of Spanish American independence had little such personal inheritance on which to draw. The Spaniards born in America were almost, if not quite, excluded from the work of government. Even the *cabildo*, the town council, failed, as a local unit of government, to maintain its representative character.[1] There was little real comparison between the Spanish *cabildo abierto*, a meeting of the town council reinforced by the principal citizenry, and the New England town-meeting; there was none at all between the government of an English colony and the organization of a Spanish viceroyalty or captaincy-general. In the *cabildos*, however, the creoles found some outlet for their ambitions, and the *cabildos* were to play a leading part in the movement for independence.

But it was not merely in administration that the Spaniards born in America were placed in a humiliating, because inferior, position, a position still harder to bear with the development among them of a moderately wealthy,

[1] It is sometimes argued that the *cabildos* 'constantly asserted their freedom', that 'in these municipalities there was no stagnation; political life was always robust and active': Cecil Jane, *Liberty and Despotism in Spanish America* (Oxford, Clarendon Press, 1929), pp. 56–7. But these assertions do not bear examination. On the colonial *cabildo* see Belaunde, op. cit., pp. 2–7.

moderately educated creole *bourgeoisie*.[1] Trade was also rigidly restricted and controlled in the interests of a few favoured centres and groups in the Americas and in those of the privileged merchants of the mother country. Till the eighteenth century commerce between Spain and her mainland colonies was generally confined to two Spanish and three colonial ports—Cartagena, Porto Bello, and Vera Cruz—and supply, except for occasional postal ships or specially licensed vessels, to the supposedly annual sailings of the galleons to Tierra Firme and the *flotas* to New Spain. The great fair at Porto Bello was intended to supply not only Central America but all South America as well, and goods for Buenos Aires travelled across the isthmus of Panamá, by sea to Callao, and overland from Lima southwards.[2] The trade of the Indies was subjected to a double monopoly, of the Seville merchants and of the commercial houses of Mexico City and Lima; and a few thousand tons supposedly sufficed for the supply of all Spain's vast dominions.

But the so-called self-sufficient empires of the English, the French, and the Spanish were never really self-sufficient, and Spain's least of all. Spain lacked the economic organization successfully to apply a monopolistic system. The stream of gold and silver which flowed from the New World itself contributed to the perversion of her economic development, and she failed to participate in the commercial expansion of Europe.[3] In Spain the fleets and galleons were loaded with

[1] On the intellectual life of the creoles and on the state of the colonial universities in particular see J. T. Lanning, *Academic Culture in the Spanish Colonies* (New York, Oxford Univ. Press, 1940).

[2] See C. H. Haring, *Trade and Navigation between Spain and the Indies in the Time of the Hapsburgs* (Harvard Univ. Press, 1918), pp. 138–9; and R. A. Humphreys, *British Consular Reports on the Trade and Politics of Latin America, 1824–1826* (Camden Third Series, lxiii, Royal Historical Society, London, 1940), p. 28, note 2; p. 111, note 2; and pp. 352–3.

[3] *Documentos para la Historia Argentina* (Facultad de Filosofía y Letras,

foreign, not Spanish, goods.[1] Their sailings became highly irregular, their tonnage much reduced, and the whole system was abolished in 1740, though the *flotas* were later temporarily revived.[2] In the colonies the most pernicious results of the system were the raising of the price-level to extravagant heights and the demonstration of the utter inadequacy of legitimate sources of supply. When the galleons sailed for the last time in 1737, they were unable to dispose of their goods because the markets were already overstocked. The smuggler and the interloper had reaped the profits which should have gone to Spain. Cause and effect moved in a vicious circle. The more debilitated Spain became the greater grew the contraband; the more the contraband, the greater Spain's debility and the weaker her empire. The illicit trade was gradually extended from the Caribbean to the South Atlantic and from the Atlantic to the Pacific. What Jamaica was to the Spanish Main the Portuguese settlement of Colonia was to Buenos Aires, and from Colonia contraband goods reached the heart of Peru. Early in the eighteenth century the South Sea Company, with the right, gained at Utrecht in 1713, to send an annual ship to the Spanish Main, its negro packet-boats, its factories, and its agents, extended and deepened the channels of contraband. Later, the free ports established by Great Britain in Jamaica and Dominica, and extended after 1787 to other strategic points in the West Indies, served still further to tap the resources and supply the needs of the Spanish colonies, and to protect a trade which in British

Buenos Aires, 1913–), v (1915), p. xxiv; A. P. Whitaker, 'The Commerce of Louisiana and the Floridas at the end of the Eighteenth Century', *Hispanic American Historical Review*, viii (1928), pp. 190–203; E. J. Hamilton, *American Treasure and the Price Revolution in Spain, 1501–1650* (Harvard Univ. Press, 1934), pp. 44–5.

[1] Haring, op. cit., p. 113.
[2] Humphreys, op. cit., pp. 352–3.

eyes was legal, in Spanish not only a crime,[1] but, as a royal decree declared in 1776, a sin![2]

It is true that Spain, like Britain, undertook in the eighteenth century the task of imperial reorganization. The administrative, economic, and educational reforms of Charles III breathed new life into the imperial system. Its administrative organization was overhauled, the Viceroyalty of La Plata was created, in 1776, out of the unwieldy Viceroyalty of Peru and the Captaincy-General of Chile, and an intendant system introduced, on the French model. Already by 1740 the fleets and galleons had died a natural death, and a beginning had been made, through the practice of licensing single vessels to trade with particular ports, in opening up the natural trade-routes of the Indies. Now, Spanish ports, other than Cádiz and Seville, were permitted to trade with the Americas; tonnage and other duties were reduced; mail services established. In 1774 the oppressive restrictions on inter-colonial commerce were lightened, and Buenos Aires, in 1776, was permitted, for the first time, to trade with the other American colonies. Finally, in 1778, by the so-called Decree of Free Trade, all the more important South American ports, on the Pacific as well as the Atlantic, were allowed to trade with the qualified ports in Spain.[3]

[1] Ibid., p. 29, note 1; p. 77, note 1; pp. 255–7. See also A. S. Aiton, 'The Asiento Treaty as reflected in the Papers of Lord Shelburne', *Hispanic American Historical Review*, viii (1928), pp. 167–77; V. L. Brown, 'Contraband Trade: A Factor in the Decline of Spain's Empire in America', ibid., pp. 178–89; and Miss Brown's earlier article, 'The South Sea Company and Contraband Trade', *American Historical Review*, xxxi (1926), pp. 662–78; A. Christelow, 'Contraband Trade between Jamaica and the Spanish Main, and the Free Port Act of 1776', *Hispanic American Historical Review*, xxii (1942), pp. 309–43; D. B. Goebel, 'British Trade to the Spanish Colonies, 1796–1823', *American Historical Review*, xliii (1938), pp. 289–94.

[2] *Documentos para la Historia Argentina*, v. 380.

[3] Humphreys, op. cit., pp. 111, 353; Ricardo Levene, *A History of Argentina* (trans. and ed. by W. S. Robertson, Chapel Hill, Univ. of North Carolina Press, 1937), pp. 106–8.

The effects of these reforms were immediate and striking. Between 1753 and 1783 the volume of trade between Spain and her colonies more than doubled. The dependence of Buenos Aires on Lima was broken, and the life of the colony was transformed.[1] The reforms stimulated an efflorescence of colonial society, a greater economic activity, an increasing regional self-consciousness. They contributed, with subsequent events, to a freer play of ideas, of which the foundation of clubs and newspapers at the end of the century was a sign; and they made yet more glaring the anomalies in the imperial structure and yet more odious the efforts of the merchants of the mother country and in the colonies to maintain a monopolistic control.

But they came too late to save the empire. Spanish America was first stimulated by one of the most enlightened of Spanish administrations; it was then misgoverned by one of the worst; and what chance, even in favourable circumstances, the reforms of Charles III might have had of averting disaster vanished when in 1796 Spain went to war with England and, with a brief interval, remained at war for twelve years more. This was the crisis of the Spanish Empire. Britain was mistress of the seas. Spain and her empire were severed. The colonists were thrown upon their own, and foreign, resources. At Buenos Aires the exports and the revenue were temporarily shattered. The Crown was forced to open commerce to neutrals, and American ships were swift to take advantage.[2] The empire, moreover, was now exposed to direct attack, and it was now Britain's turn to dally with the idea of the independence of colonies.

[1] *Documentos para la Historia Argentina*, v, pp. xxxvii–xxxix; Humphreys, op. cit., p. 29, note 2; Levene, op. cit., p. 109.

[2] Humphreys, op. cit., p. 30, note 3; p. 31, note 1; p. 46, note 1; *Documentos para la Historia Argentina*, vii (1916), p. 134; A. P. Whitaker, *The United States and the Independence of Latin America, 1800–1830* (Baltimore, Johns Hopkins Press, 1941), pp. 8–16, 23–6.

In 1797 the Governor of Trinidad was instructed to promote measures to liberate the Spanish colonies, with the assurance that if they revolted they would receive British aid.[1] In 1806, after the renewal of war between England and Spain, Sir Home Popham, on his own responsibility, undertook to invade the River Plate. For nearly three months Buenos Aires was in British hands, and the fact that, after the Viceroy had fled, the British forces were expelled by the creoles themselves resounded throughout South America and stirred creole blood everywhere. In the following year a relief expedition captured Montevideo and again advanced upon Buenos Aires. This expedition also was forced to capitulate. But Great Britain entertained little serious idea of conquest in South America; her policy was commercial rather than imperial; and in 1808 the army which Wellesley was preparing in Ireland was designed for the emancipation of Spanish America, not its subjugation.

Suddenly, however, the situation was transformed. Napoleon's invasion of the Peninsula converted Spain from an enemy to an ally of England; Wellesley sailed not to liberate Spanish America from Spain but to liberate Spain from France; and the Napoleonic invasion of Spain precipitated the revolutions of Spanish American independence. The nationalist, monarchist movement in Spain was paralleled by a semi-nationalist, semi-monarchist movement in Spanish America. On the famous 2 May 1808 the people of Madrid revolted against the troops of Napoleon. This was the prelude to the national uprising against the invader. In Spanish America the news of the abdication of Charles IV, the renunciation of Ferdinand the Well-Beloved, and the accession of Joseph Bonaparte was received with a fervour of loyal indignation. When the agents of Napoleon arrived

[1] W. S. Robertson, *The Life of Miranda* (2 vols., Chapel Hill, Univ. of North Carolina Press, 1929), i. 161; Levene, op. cit., p. 193.

at Caracas they were driven from the city by an infuriated mob; his emissary to Buenos Aires was expelled by the Porteños and imprisoned by the authorities at Montevideo. Superficially the movement in Spain was exactly imitated in Spanish America. As juntas sprang up in Spain in the name of Ferdinand VII, so Ferdinand's accession was solemnly proclaimed in Spanish America, and the juntas which were there established in 1809–10 acknowledged his authority.

But the colonies were Crown colonies. The Crown, and presumably its agents, had fallen into the hands of France. Power, it could be argued, and was argued, had therefore reverted to the people. From this there was no going back. As the English colonies in North America in the eighteenth century, victorious in their long struggle to establish their supremacy over the instruments of the royal prerogative, refused to accept the sovereignty of Parliament, so the Spanish colonies, when the Crown was incapacitated, refused to accept subordination to the people of the Peninsula. Juntas and *cabildos* assumed the powers of viceroys, presidents, and captains-general; and what began as an assertion of freedom from French control ended as a war of independence from Spain.

It is true that the Regency in Spain invited the Americans to attend the Cortes which met in Cádiz in 1810 and which adopted the Liberal Constitution of 1812. But the Peninsular Spaniards clung to the principle of subordination. The creoles were denied equal or proportionate representation in the Cortes. Their demands for freedom of trade were rejected. Other of their petitions were brushed aside.[1] Castlereagh, in 1812, clearly perceived the end. Unless, he wrote, Spain was prepared to place

[1] A. F. Zimmerman, 'Spain and its Colonies, 1808–1820', *Hispanic American Historical Review*, xi (1931), pp. 446–9.

'the inhabitants of America upon a commercial footing of corresponding advantage with the inhabitants of European Spain, and that without loss of time, their separation from the Parent State is inevitable and at hand. . . . Provinces of such magnitude will not longer submit to be treated as mere colonies. They have not only in point of fact outgrown that relation, but they have been acknowledged by the Cortes to be no longer dependent Colonies, but integral parts of the Spanish monarchy, equal in rights, and admissible upon that principle to an equal share in the national representation.'[1]

But that equality, at first theoretically admitted, was in fact denied. Spain, like Britain, was unable to conceive of a Commonwealth of Nations united by allegiance to the Crown. It did not need the restoration of Ferdinand VII, and despotism, in 1814, to make independence ultimately sure.

Meanwhile the empire disintegrated, along the lines of old judicial and administrative divisions. It was not a simple process. Almost everywhere it was complicated and embittered by regional and personal rivalries, by divergences of aims and opinions, and by conflicts both of interests and ideas between the Old Spaniards, the office-holders and monopolists, and the creoles, and between the creoles themselves. As Sarmiento observed, of the revolutionary process in Argentina, moreover, it was 'interesting and intelligible' only to the cities, but 'foreign and unmeaning to the rural districts', except as it meant a shaking off of royal and judicial authority. The Argentine revolutionary war, he declared, was twofold, a civilized warfare of the cities against Spain, and a war against the cities on the part of the country chieftains. 'These Spartan constitutions [of the gauchos], that war-like nature hitherto ill-satisfied by the free use of the dagger, that Roman-like idleness which could only be exchanged for the activity of a battle-field, that

[1] Webster, op. cit. ii. 311.

utter impatience of judicial control, were all to have at last
a fit sphere of action in the world.'[1]

Already in 1809 at Chuquisaca (the modern Sucre,
Bolivia), long famous as the seat of the *audiencia* of Charcas,
of an archbishopric, and of a university, the *audiencia* had
deposed its President; at La Paz, in the same Presidency,
the intendant was overthrown; and in the Presidency of
Quito, the President was removed and imprisoned in his
own capital. The first of these movements was inspired by
the judicial authorities and the university; the second by
radical and mestizo elements in the city; and the third
by the local creole aristocracy.[2] All were sternly repressed
from Peru, the home of a privileged nobility and the strong-
hold of Spanish wealth and power. But in 1810 the *cabildo*
at Caracas deposed the Captain-General of Venezuela. At
Buenos Aires, on the famous 25 May, the Viceroy of La
Plata was supplanted. At Santa Fé de Bogotá an extraordinary *cabildo* established a junta for the Viceroyalty
of New Granada. At Santiago de Chile the Captain-
General was forced to resign, and a *cabildo abierto* elected
a provisional junta to rule the colony during the captivity
of Ferdinand VII.

In each case these new authorities proclaimed their
loyalty to the Crown. It was not, indeed, till 1816 that 'the
United Provinces of South America' (Argentina) declared
their independence. But the revolution of 25 May 1810 at
Buenos Aires was in effect, if not in formal fact, a declaration of independence. The British invasions had intensified
the political ferment and the economic conflict in Buenos
Aires between the partisans of a new and those of an old
order. The Viceroy had fled; the port had been opened to

[1] D. F. Sarmiento, *Life in the Argentine Republic in the Days of the Tyrants;
or Civilization and Barbarism* (trans. Mrs. Horace Mann, New York, 1868),
pp. 56–7, 62.   [2] Belaunde, op. cit., pp. 95–6.

British commerce. Though a new Viceroy was appointed, the Porteños were politically transformed; and despite the efforts of the monopolists, the port was never completely closed again.[1] The revolution was the direct outcome of these conditions; and the Porteños were prepared not only to defend their new independence *de facto* against the constituted authorities in Montevideo, but to extend their rule, if they could, over the whole of the Viceroyalty of La Plata, including the provinces which now form Bolivia, Paraguay, and Uruguay. High up the Paraguay, however, the creoles of Asunción had no intention of exchanging the sovereignty of Spain for that of Buenos Aires, and in 1811 they carried out their own revolution, deposing the Governor and establishing a junta, of which one member was the redoubtable Dr. José Gaspar Rodríguez de Francia, who, in 1813, became one of the two consuls of the Republic of Paraguay and in 1814 its dictator. In 1811 also Artigas, in the Banda Oriental of Uruguay, raised the standard of revolt against the royalists in Montevideo and was prepared to fight against them, the Portuguese from Brazil, or the Porteños, impartially. Finally, in 1811 Venezuela was the first of the future republics to proclaim its independence; a Congress was called in Chile; another, in New Granada, announced the formation of the United Provinces of New Granada; and Cartagena declared that it had become an independent state.

Within five years these movements appeared everywhere to have been crushed, except in the River Plate. In Chile the patriots, torn by internecine strife, were subjugated from Peru. In Venezuela Miranda, the first dictator, had been forced to capitulate to the royalists in 1812, and the young Bolívar, who entered the service of the junta at Cartagena, marched from Cartagena to Caracas, again

[1] Humphreys, op. cit., p. 31, note 2.

expelled the royalists and was proclaimed Liberator, had to flee the country in 1814. New Granada had been reconquered by an army of Peninsular veterans, in 1816. Only in the former Viceroyalty of La Plata did the revolution survive, and there, in Buenos Aires, governments had succeeded governments with bewildering rapidity, while, across the River Plate, the Banda Oriental was a scene of chaos and war.

This was the critical year of the revolutionary wars. The reaction in 1816 was at its height; the cause was in the balance. Then, in December, Bolívar began his final campaign for the liberation of his country. In 1817 he formed his capital at Angostura (now Ciudad Bolívar) and in 1819 led his army over heights of 13,000 feet to liberate New Granada and to form in 1821 the Republic of (Great) Colombia. In the south, José de San Martín, who had been quietly organizing his Army of the Andes at Mendoza, in January 1817 suddenly crossed the mountain barrier by a pass more than 12,000 feet above sea-level, to fall upon the royalists in Chile. Finally, in the ships of the new republic, he sailed with his veteran army to proclaim in Lima, in July 1821, the independence of Peru.

In this epic story, which has the Homeric quality of the conquest itself, the figures of Bolívar and San Martín stand supreme, as victors and organizers of victory. It is they who give to the wars of independence in South America what formal unity they may have; and when the two men met in their mysterious interview at Guayaquil in July 1822, the liberating stream from the north, which drew its strength from Caracas, and that from the south, which drew its strength from Buenos Aires, were joined. Thereafter San Martín, with much self-abnegation, withdrew, to leave the field clear for Bolívar. 'I have witnessed', he wrote, 'the declaration of independence of the states of Chile and Peru

... and I have ceased to be a public man. Thus I am recompensed with usury for ten years employed in revolution and in war. My promise to the countries for which I have fought is fulfilled: to secure their independence, and to leave them to select their own governments.' 'The presence', he added, 'of a fortunate soldier, however disinterested he may be, is dangerous to newly established states.'[1] Meanwhile, Peru, having been ruled by an Argentine protector, a native junta of three, and two native presidents, appointed Bolívar, in February 1824, its dictator. Guayaquil and Quito had already been added to Colombia. It remained for Bolívar's lieutenant, Sucre, to defeat the last Spanish Viceroy at 'the crowning mercy' of Ayacucho on 9 December 1824, and South America was free.

In North and Middle America the revolution took a somewhat different course. In Mexico itself the viceregal authority was maintained almost as long as in Peru. There, after an abortive creole attempt to form a junta in 1808 and a rapid succession of viceroys, an Indian and mestizo revolt in 1810 showed what dangerous forces revolution might unleash. The revolt was still not entirely crushed at the time of the Liberal revolution of 1820 in Spain, when, highly alarmed by this last event, the Spaniards in Mexico determined to save New Spain from the dangerous innovations of Old Spain. They found an instrument in a young creole, Agustín de Iturbide; but Iturbide, sent to quell the guerrilla leaders, made terms with them, declared the independence of Mexico, and was proclaimed emperor in May 1822, only to be forced to fly the country within ten months. A Constitution on the model of that of the United States was then adopted, and the first President of the Mexican Republic was inaugurated in October 1824.

Farther south, an assembly at Guatemala City, infected

[1] Levene, op. cit., p. 324.

by the news of events in Spain and Mexico, declared the independence of the old Captaincy-General of Guatemala in September 1821. For a brief period Iturbide in Mexico was successful in extending his authority from Guatemala to Panamá, but, on the news of his downfall, an assembly representing the five provinces of Costa Rica, Guatemala, Honduras, Nicaragua, and Salvador met, and on 1 July 1823 declared that these were independent states confederated as the United Provinces of Central America—a confederation never united except in name.

One fortunate country, Brazil, escaped the convulsions which shook her neighbours. To Brazil the Portuguese royal family had fled in 1807–8, escorted by British warships. Rio de Janeiro, which had not long supplanted Bahia as the capital of Brazil, now supplanted Lisbon as the capital of Portugal. In matters of commerce Brazil had never been quite so harshly treated by Portugal as Spanish America by Spain. But now in 1808 the ports of Brazil were thrown open to the trade of the world, although in 1810 the commercial privileges which Britain had enjoyed in Portugal were duplicated, or almost duplicated, in Brazil. 'New people, new capital, and ideas entered.'[1] In 1815, moreover, the colony was raised to the rank of a kingdom, co-equal with Portugal; and from that there could be no descent again to colonial status. But the Crown could not permanently remain in exile, and in 1821 Dom João I, King of Portugal, Brazil, and the Algarves, reluctantly returned home, leaving his son, Pedro, as regent in Brazil. But the Cortes in Portugal, like the Cortes in Spain, had learnt nothing and forgotten nothing. Its efforts to reduce Brazil to its former status could have but one result. On 7 September 1822 Dom Pedro, placing himself at the head

[1] A. K. Manchester, *British Preëminence in Brazil. Its Rise and Decline* (Chapel Hill, Univ. of North Carolina Press, 1933), pp. 70–2.

of the independent party in Brazil, declared for 'independence or death'. On 12 October he was officially proclaimed Emperor of Brazil. The few Portuguese troops in the country were forced to withdraw, and in 1824 Pedro promulgated the Liberal Constitution which survived, with modifications, till 1889. Finally, through the efforts of Great Britain, Portugal, in 1825, recognized the independence of Brazil, though it was not till 1836 that Spain began the process of recognizing her former colonies and not till 1895 that she completed it.

By 1830, when Bolívar died, like San Martín, in exile, the territorial divisions of the Latin American map had more or less assumed their modern form. Out of war between Brazil and Buenos Aires, and through the mediation of Great Britain, the independent state of Uruguay had been born in 1828. The independence of Bolivia was proclaimed three years earlier, and in 1830 Bolívar's great Colombian federation dissolved into its component parts of Ecuador, New Granada, and Venezuela.

The continent was free, and it was no longer closed. Already in 1810 the revolutionary juntas had hastened to throw open the ports of South America to the ships and commerce of the world. In Chile and Venezuela the reconquest closed them, but only for a space. In the last days of Spanish rule even the Viceroy of Peru was compelled to connive at foreign trade, and even in Cuba a royal decree in 1818 declared the ports open. The transition from illegal to legal trade, from the closed to the open door, was complete,[1] and a new migration of men and money from the Old World to the New had already begun. There was, it is true, little to support Canning's contention that in 1810, when British mediation between Spain and her colonies

[1] Humphreys, op. cit., p. x; D. B. Goebel, 'British Trade to the Spanish Colonies, 1796–1823', *American Historical Review*, xliii (1938), pp. 288–320.

was asked for by Spain, and granted by Britain, permission to trade with America was given by Spain in return.[1] But Britain had begun to trade, and that trade she would not forgo. British and American ships touched at every port. The continent was flooded with British goods. The legend of the golden market replaced the legend of the golden man. So frenzied was the zeal for export that warming-pans and skates were sent to Rio de Janeiro and Montevideo.[2] There was even an association for exporting milkmaids to Buenos Aires, while the orgy of speculation in England in 1824–5 in South American mines rivalled the days of the South Sea Bubble. In England, moreover, the young republics sought money and credit, and in England at the beginning of the nineteenth century, as in the United States at the end, capital looked abroad. Latin America was a new and apparently a fertile field, and already by 1825 more than twenty million pounds sterling, one way or another, had been there invested.[3]

The Latin American peoples won their own independence. Nothing can detract from that achievement. But the resources of British merchants and bankers and the services of British volunteers on land and sea afforded invaluable aid to the insurgents. The record of Lord Cochrane in Chile and Brazil and of the men of the British and Irish legions who served under Bolívar is not forgotten in Latin America. It is true that after 1808 Great Britain did not actively promote or specifically desire the political independence of Latin America, though the sympathies of the new Liberal movement were early enlisted in that cause. Like the United States, Britain followed a policy of correct

---

[1] Humphreys, op. cit., p. 257, note 2.

[2] Ibid., p. 32, note 1; R. Walsh, *Notices of Brazil in 1828 and 1829* (2 vols., London, 1830), i. 443; Manning, *Diplomatic Correspondence*, i. 454.

[3] L. H. Jenks, *The Migration of British Capital to 1875* (London, Cape, 1938), p. 64.

neutrality. She was prepared to mediate on liberal terms between Spain and her colonies. But she was not prepared to see the continent again closed to British commerce. Nor was she prepared to tolerate intervention by the European Powers in Latin American affairs. In a famous memorandum of 20 August 1817, Castlereagh made the position of Great Britain absolutely clear. Mediation, yes, on liberal terms; but force should never be employed against the Spanish colonies by any other Power than Spain.[1] With that resolve on the part of the world's greatest naval Power, the independence of Latin America was assured. What Castlereagh had done was to remove the possibility of intervention when the issue was still in doubt, and, whatever the effects of intervention might have been, the service to the infant states was immeasurable.

Once again, in 1823, when there were fears—groundless fears, as it turned out—of European intervention, Great Britain, through the energy of Canning, secured from France, the only European Power that was potentially dangerous, a disavowal of any such intention.[2] It was not, however, till 1822 that Great Britain recognized the flags of South American vessels, an act which constituted recognition *de facto*, not till 1823 that she appointed consuls in Spanish South America, and not till 1825 that, by the method of the negotiation of commercial treaties with Buenos Aires, Colombia, and Mexico, she accorded recognition *de jure*.[3]

The United States had taken earlier action. United States commercial agents appeared in Spanish America

[1] Webster, op. cit. i. 14; ii. 352–8.

[2] Ibid. i. 19. The whole subject of French designs is discussed in W. S. Robertson, *France and Latin-American Independence* (Baltimore, Johns Hopkins Press, 1939).

[3] Difficulties arose over the Mexican treaty. It was not ratified by the British Government and a new treaty was negotiated in 1826.

before the revolution began. United States consuls were appointed long before British. As early as 1817 commissioners were dispatched to inquire into the state of South American affairs. But their reports were confused and discouraging. The United States was then engaged in delicate negotiations with Spain, which led to Spain's cession of the Floridas, and these negotiations were not brought to their certain and triumphant conclusion till 1821. John Quincy Adams, moreover, the greatest of American Secretaries of State, inherently cautious and firmly attached to legal and moral principles, studiously attempted to follow a policy of correct neutrality. He would, it is true, have been ready in 1819 to have acted with England in joint recognition of Buenos Aires; but recognition was only one aspect of a complex diplomatic situation, and Castlereagh had other views. Adams was not prepared to act alone. By 1821, however, the situation had changed. The Florida Treaty was ratified. In South America the revolutionaries were everywhere successful. The United States hesitated no longer; in 1822 it acted swiftly and it acted alone, the first of the Powers to recognize the independence of the Latin American states.

There were many points of similarity in the policies pursued by Great Britain and the United States. In both countries the official attitude was cautious, but in both there was a large body of Liberal and commercial opinion on the side of the insurgents. Both pursued a policy that was commercial rather than imperial. Neither, with certain exceptions, of which the chief was the privileged position obtained by Great Britain in Brazil, sought exclusive commercial advantages. Both were resolved to prevent the partition of Latin America by other Powers. But while they were conscious of a certain community of purpose, they were conscious also of great differences between them. Republics were admired in the New World and disliked in the Old. Castlereagh would have been glad to see Bourbon monarchs at the head of the new states.[1] Canning viewed the preservation of the principle of monarchy in Brazil as the culminating point of his grand design to link the new states to Europe and Europe to the new states. To these ideas the United States was ineradicably opposed. The incompatibility of the European and American systems was a fundamental point in the Monroe Doctrine; it was an American system and an American policy that the United States wished to see predominate. Both Britain and the United States, moreover, feared the territorial expansion of the other. On the Spanish borderlands, in the peripheral provinces, indeed, the expansion of the United States was a contributory element to the fall of the Spanish Empire;[2] and Adams and Canning each suspected, though with little justification, the other's designs on Cuba. Finally, to political rivalry, there was added also commercial hostility.[3]

In this atmosphere, in December 1823, the Monroe Doctrine was born. By that master-stroke of national policy, Adams, taking advantage of the offer made by Canning for joint protection of the Latin American states against European intervention, appeared to elevate the United States to the position of arbiter of the New World. Never had opportunity been turned to more brilliant advantage. It was not that the doctrine gave official sanction to 'the idea that the United States would, if necessary, fight for the independence of a foreign nation'.[4] The brilliance lay in the use to which the knowledge that there

---

[1] Webster, op. cit. i. 17.

[2] C. C. Griffin, *The United States and the Disruption of the Spanish Empire 1810–1822* (New York, Columbia Univ. Press, 1937), pp. 16 ff.

[3] See J. F. Rippy, *Rivalry of the United States and Great Britain over Latin America, 1808–1830* (Baltimore, Johns Hopkins Press, 1929).

[4] Whitaker, op. cit., p. 518.

would be no need to fight was put.[1] The commercial treaties of 1825 were Canning's riposte, and by 1826 Canning had secured that everywhere in Latin America Great Britain was regarded as the Power most important for the security and prosperity of the new states.

The Monroe Doctrine was important not for what it did but for what it became. But behind it and the silent support of British naval power the infant states were to be left to work out their own destinies. The familiar pattern, cause of so many wars, of a disintegrating area subject to partition by the European Powers was not here to be repeated. Latin America, which was, in the nineteenth century, a frontier of Europe, was also an American continent, and the freedom which the Latin American peoples had won was theirs to organize in their own way.

[1] Cf. Webster, op. cit. i. 49–50.

III

THE COMING OF THE IMMIGRANT

FROM southern Brazil to southern Patagonia is the 'pioneer hinterland'[1] of South America. Buenos Aires, in 1776, when it became the capital of the newly created Viceroyalty of La Plata, was a small provincial town with a population of about 24,000, situated in an area the least valued by Spain of all her colonial possessions in the Americas. A quarter of a century later, on the eve of the establishment of its independence, it numbered perhaps 45,000 souls.[2] To-day, with a population of $3\frac{1}{2}$ millions, greater Buenos Aires is the third city of the western hemisphere. Montevideo, in the eighteen-twenties, counted hardly more than 10,000 inhabitants.[3] As for São Paulo, even in the eighteen-sixties it was still a small town of about 25,000 people.[4]

The coming of the immigrant, and of foreign capital, transformed this area, formerly the poorest, into the richest and most prosperous part of South America. For three centuries, under Spanish and Portuguese rule, Latin America was in theory, and to a considerable extent in practice, a closed continent. Immigration, like trade, was restricted and controlled in the interests of the mother countries. There was a brief period, in the reign of Charles V, when the Spanish Crown permitted its non-Spanish subjects to emigrate to the New World. Thenceforth, the Indies were closed. The English, the Dutch, and the French were compelled by Spain's pre-emptive claims

---

[1] Bowman, *The Pioneer Fringe*, p. 3.
[2] Humphreys, *British Consular Reports*, p. 18, note 2.
[3] Ibid., p. 76, note 2.
[4] W. Hadfield, *Brazil and the River Plate in 1868* (London, 1869), p. 67.

to turn their attention to North America, to such islands as they could obtain in the West Indies, and to the Guianas. Only a few Europeans other than Spaniards penetrated to the mainland colonies of Spain, though a long series of royal decrees complaining both of foreigners and of foreign goods reveals their presence.[1]

But with the opening of the ports of Latin America to the ships and commerce of the world, the immigrant followed the trader. The emancipation of so vast an area deeply stirred the imaginations of men, and enthusiasm was proportionate to ignorance. 'He must indeed be more than temperate, he must be a cold reasoner,' said Brougham in 1817, 'who can glance at those regions and not grow warm.' In England the printing-presses were flooded with literature on the southern continent, much of it highly coloured, and for a brief space Latin America took precedence of the United States as the land of hope and promise.

The new states themselves needed men and money, and both were sought abroad. Paraguay, under Dr. Francia (whom Carlyle characteristically discovered and admired), was, it is true, a country barely possible to enter and nearly impossible to leave. But the United Provinces of the Río de la Plata established an immigration commission in 1824, and in that year the 'Unemployed Poor of Great Britain and Ireland' were invited, on generous terms, to settle on the lands of the Río de la Plata Agricultural Association in Entre Ríos. A few hundred unfortunates, English and some German, thus found themselves involved in disaster.[2] A more judicious enterprise, in the same year, for the establishment of an agricultural colony at Monte Grande, not far from Buenos Aires, was temporarily more successful. In

---

[1] Cf. *Documentos para la Historia Argentina*, v, pp. 73, 375; vii, p. lxxxii.

[2] See J. A. B. Beaumont, *Travels in Buenos Ayres and the Adjacent Provinces* (London, 1828).

this case the immigrants, mostly from the west and south of Scotland, were chosen 'with a view at once to their agricultural skill and their religious and moral character'; and it is saying a good deal that the colony held together till 1829.[1] In Chile the Government proposed, in 1825, to settle a colony of Irish peasants on lands to the south of the Bío-Bío, at that time exposed to the ravages of the Araucanian Indians.[2] In Brazil an unsuccessful Swiss colony was established at New Freiburg, near Rio de Janeiro, in 1818, and the first German settlement in Rio Grande do Sul, at São Leopoldo, north of Porto Alegre, took place in 1824. Four years later Robert Owen solicited the Government of Mexico to cede to him Coahuila and Texas as 'the most desirable point on the Globe' on which to establish a 'model government for the general benefit of all other governments and people but more immediately, for the benefit of the South and North American Republics'.[3]

Merchants and traders, meanwhile, thronged to the seaports. When in 1807 Montevideo temporarily fell into British hands (while Britain was at war with Spain) some six thousand British subjects were reported to have entered the town, 'of whom four thousand were military, two thousand merchants, traders, adventurers; and a dubious crew which could scarcely pass muster, even under the latter designation'.[4] The British community in Buenos Aires

[1] James Dodds, *Records of the Scottish Settlers in the River Plate and their Churches* (Buenos Aires, 1897), pp. 3–62.   [2] Humphreys, op. cit., pp. 168–9.
[3] Memorial of Robert Owen to the Mexican Republic, Sept. 1828. I am indebted to the courtesy of Sr. Don Rafael Heliodoro Valle and to the University of Texas for a transcript of this document from the Archives of the Mexican Ministry of Foreign Affairs. The petition was forwarded by the Mexican Chargé d'Affaires in London with the comment 'aunque es muy hermoso, muy plausible y muy filantrópico en el papel, es inverificable en la práctica'.
[4] J. P. and W. P. Robertson, *Letters on Paraguay* (3 vols., 2nd edn., London, 1839), i. 102.

took root between 1808 and 1810, after the failure of these British invasions of the River Plate, and already by 1824 nearly 3,000 British subjects were there resident. Their number had grown to more than 4,000 by 1830, and in 1832 Woodbine Parish, the first British Minister to the United Provinces of the Río de la Plata, estimated that there were between 15,000 and 20,000 foreigners in Buenos Aires and the Province of Buenos Aires, of whom about two-thirds were French and British in equal proportions.[1] Valparaíso, in Chile, was reported in 1822 to resemble a 'coast town in Britain', and, as a jaundiced traveller observed, to be 'full of English, many of them of the lowest description and of the worst characters'.[2] Even Lima contained, by 1824, some 250 British residents,[3] while in Mexico City, in 1826, besides a few English and American commercial houses, there was said to be an 'immense number' of foreign shopkeepers, principally French.[4] As for Rio de Janeiro, when H.M. ship *Cambridge* arrived there in 1824, taking out the first British consuls to Spanish America, her chaplain reported the presence of 100 English merchants and four English shopkeepers, 'and the same number of French; but in the reverse order, namely, four merchants and 100 shop-keepers'.[5]

But from these beginnings the growth of immigration was slow. The movement of capital and people to the Mississippi valley and to southern Brazil and Argentina was part and parcel of the same great process, the rising

[1] Humphreys, op. cit., p. 26, note 2; Woodbine Parish, *Buenos Ayres and the Provinces of the Rio de la Plata* (1st edn., London, 1839), p. 30.

[2] Humphreys, op. cit., p. 91, note 1.

[3] Ibid., p. 108, note 1.   [4] Ibid., p. 303, note 2.

[5] *Journal written on Board of His Majesty's Ship Cambridge from January, 1824, to May, 1827*. By the Rev. H. S., Chaplain (Newcastle, 1829), p. 17. See also Maria Graham, *Journal of a Voyage to Brazil* . . . (London, 1824), p. 189.

importance of the Atlantic basin. It was a chapter both in the political and economic history of South America and in the political and economic history of Europe. But though, in the nineteenth century, Latin America, like the United States, was a European 'frontier', an investment and an immigration 'frontier', it was only towards the end of the century that immigration took place on any considerable scale. Large parts of the continent remained untouched by the immigrant stream, and at no time did migration to Latin America equal the great migration to the United States.

The first flush of enthusiasm in the eighteen-twenties, indeed, quickly paled, and disenchantment followed. Reports of political disorder and economic insecurity, the embittered accounts of unfortunate speculators, a more exact knowledge of social and physical conditions, discouraged all but the boldest or the most deluded; and it was true that countries such as Peru or Bolivia or even Mexico had little to offer but illusions. 'To govern', wrote the great Argentine publicist, J. B. Alberdi, 'is to populate', and the Argentine Constitution of 1853, which owed so much to Alberdi, specifically enjoined upon the Federal Government the duty of promoting European immigration. The Constitution is a watershed in Argentine history. But Sarmiento's famous book, *Facundo*, written in 1845, accurately reflects the turbulence of life in Argentina before that 'Great Divide' was reached, and its sub-title, *Civilisation and Barbarism*, speaks for itself.

The immigrant stream, therefore, set to the northern rather than the southern continent, and the United States, with its abundance of cheap land, became, and remained, the Utopia of the immigrant. With the Homestead Act of 1862, a wise and far-sighted public land policy there set the pattern of rural expansion. Latin America also had land.

But there was no legislation in Latin America strictly comparable to the homestead legislation of the United States. On the contrary, the system of landholding still prevalent in most Latin American countries restricted the possibilities of settlement and maintained the status of the agricultural labourer at a level far below that prevailing in most European countries. It may well be that in remote and thinly peopled areas the *hacienda*, the great landed estate, was, and perhaps still is, the most practicable social and economic unit, and the plantation system the only possible means of agriculture. Certainly they made possible the exploitation of land which must otherwise have remained unworked and unsettled. But the *hacienda*, as a way of life and labour, and land monopoly, survived also even in areas where their influence was almost wholly bad and where new conditions made necessary a new economy.[1] As late as 1925 in the Province of Aconcagua, in the rich Central Valley of Chile, 98 per cent. of the farm land was comprised in 3 per cent. of the rural properties.[2] In Mexico, on the eve of the revolution of 1910, of the population that tilled the soil 95 per cent. owned none of it.[3] In Brazil, in 1920, 90 per cent. of the occupied agricultural population were wage-earners, and Argentina, in the nineteen-thirties, still remained a country of great landowners and tenant-farmers. The large holding was the rule when Argentina was a pastoral country. It was still the rule when to a pastoral economy had been added a cereal-growing economy.[4]

[1] Cf. Bowman, *The Pioneer Fringe*, pp. 299–303.

[2] McBride, *Chile: Land and Society*, p. 124.

[3] G. M. McBride, *The Land Systems of Mexico* (New York, American Geographical Society, 1923), p. 154, and E. N. Simpson, *The Ejido, Mexico's Way Out* (Chapel Hill, Univ. of North Carolina Press, 1937), pp. 32–3.

[4] R. Paula Lopes, 'Social Problems and Legislation in Brazil', *International Labour Review*, xliv (1941), p. 505; 'Immigration and Settlement in Brazil, Argentina, and Uruguay', ibid. xxxv (1937), pp. 355, 362; Bowman, *The Pioneer Fringe*, p. 303.

Only in a few areas in Latin America, notably in Costa Rica, has landownership taken the form of small holdings.

In Argentina, in southern Brazil, and even in Uruguay and Chile, however, immigration played something of the part that it played in the United States. Between 1857, when the first attempt was made to compile at least some Argentine immigration statistics, and 1930, after which restrictions on immigration were imposed, more than six million immigrants entered Argentina.[1] Some were 'birds of passage', 'golondrinas', seasonal migrants, who came to reap the harvests and then returned to their native Italy.[2] Others re-emigrated. But more than one-half found in Argentina their permanent homes. Even in 1940 nearly a fifth of the population was of foreign birth, and in 1914 the proportion was nearly one-third.[3] Brazil, between 1820 and 1930, admitted some four and a half million immigrants.[4] But so high was the rate of re-emigration that in some years the number departing from the country exceeded that of those entering. In the three southern states of Rio Grande do Sul, Santa Catarina, and Paraná, where it was almost always possible for the immigrant to acquire land, the new-comers were, for the most part, permanent settlers. But by far the largest number of emigrants to Brazil have been attracted to São Paulo, and of all those entering São Paulo between 1908 and 1935, whether from

[1] A. E. Bunge, 'Ochenta y Cinco Años de Inmigración', *Revista de Economía Argentina* (Buenos Aires), xliii (1944), pp. 31–2.

[2] See Mark Jefferson, *Peopling the Argentine Pampa* (New York, American Geographical Society, 1926), pp. 189–91.

[3] C. Luzzetti Estevarena, 'Ethnical Composition of the Population of Argentina', *Bulletin of the Pan American Union* (Nov. 1941), pp. 625–6.

[4] *Revista de Imigração e Colonização* (Rio de Janeiro), i, No. 4 (Oct. 1940); *International Migrations* (2 vols., New York, National Bureau of Economic Research, vol. i, I. Ferenczi, comp., 1929; vol. ii, W. F. Willcox, ed., 1931), ii. 163.

abroad or from other parts of Brazil, less than a half remained there.[1]

In Argentina the real beginnings of this movement were in the fifties and sixties. The Federal Constitution was adopted in 1853, and though, between 1853 and 1861, Buenos Aires was divided from the rest of the provinces and the schism was only ended by civil war, in 1861, the transformation that followed was spectacular. The first railway, the Great Western, was opened in 1857. The northern was built between 1862 and 1864, at a cost of £24,000 a mile. The Great Southern began operations in 1864–5, reaching Bahía Blanca in 1884. The Central Argentine, begun in 1863, reached Córdoba in 1870. In the fifties also the first agricultural colonies were founded. Esperanza, settled by French-speaking and German-speaking Swiss, led the way in the Province of Santa Fe in 1856, and some twenty-five others followed in the same province between 1858 and 1870. In 1856 also agricultural colonies were founded at San José in the Province of Entre Ríos and at Baradero in the Province of Buenos Aires, and in southern Patagonia the foundation of the Welsh colony of Chubut dates from 1865.

But in 1865 there were only 373 square miles of tilled land in the republic.[2] European farmers, lease-holders, and tenants on the pampa, transformed Argentina into one of the great granaries of the world; and the opening of the pampa, the growth of the railways, and the influx of people were intimately related. In 1867 there were only 319 miles of railway in Argentina. By 1892 there were 7,514 miles.[3] As late as 1875 Argentina was still a grain-importing

---

[1] Cf. R. Paula Lopes, 'Land Settlement in Brazil', *International Labour Review*, xxxiii (1936), pp. 172–3; see also 'Immigration and Settlement in Brazil, Argentina, and Uruguay', ibid. xxxv (1937), pp. 235–6.

[2] Jefferson, op. cit., p. 42.   [3] Ibid., p. 161.

country. In 1887 wheat exports alone amounted to more than 237,000 tons.[1] Ten years earlier the first refrigerator ship made its appearance; the first *frigorífico* was built in 1882; and barbed wire, as important to the Argentine pampa as to the North American plains, was invented in the seventies. Barbed wire, the refrigerator, the railway, the immigrant—on these the prosperity of modern Argentina was built; and it was in the eighties that immigration, actively encouraged by the Government, first attained to high proportions (219,000 in 1889). It reached its peak in the decade before the first World War (323,000 in 1912); and though the war years placed a temporary stoppage to this immigrant stream, there was revival in the nineteen-twenties. But the figures of the peak years of 1889 and 1912 were never again reached, and the decline in net immigration preceded the restrictive legislation of the thirties.

In Brazil, where the abolition of the slave-trade first stimulated the demand for European labour, Dom Pedro, the second Emperor of Brazil, consistently encouraged immigration, as he encouraged also, partly with a view to attract the immigrant, the building of railways, first begun in Brazil in 1854. But it was with the abolition of slavery itself, in 1888, and after the establishment of the republic, that the great expansion came, and the rapid and extraordinary growth of the coffee industry in the state of São Paulo was both the cause and the effect of mass migration. While, in the eighteen-nineties, there was a sudden and on the whole sustained fall in immigration to Argentina, then caught in the throes of a financial and economic crisis, in the decade between 1888 and 1898 more than a million and a quarter immigrants entered Brazil.[2] Yet a further

[1] L. R. Gondra, *Historia Económica de la República Argentina* (Buenos Aires, Editorial Sudamericana, 1942), p. 432.
[2] *Revista de Imigração e Colonização*, i, No. 4 (Oct. 1940).

million entered between 1904 and 1913, and between 1889 and 1915 the State of São Paulo itself paid the transportation charges of over 900,000 immigrants.[1] Thenceforth, as in Argentina, there was a relative decline, only temporarily arrested in the nineteen-twenties, and, with the advent of the world depression, Brazil, like Argentina, drastically restricted immigration.

The majority of these immigrants were Italians, Spaniards, and Portuguese, though the Spaniards naturally preferred Argentina and the Portuguese Brazil. Nearly a half of all Argentine immigrants came from Italy. One-third came from Spain. Italy and Portugal supplied two-thirds and Spain an eighth of the emigrants to Brazil. It is not difficult to understand the popularity of the Italians as immigrants. They presented few difficulties of assimilation and readily made the new lands their own, while the Spaniards, as Jefferson has noted, tended to stand aloof from the creoles.[2] They were hard-working, persevering, and easily adaptable. They were 'for the most part', wrote the Mulhalls in 1885, of the Italians in Argentina, 'laborious, sober and frugal: they are found in every walk of life, and the children of Italian fathers and Argentine mothers are remarkably intelligent.'[3] In politics, law, and commerce, the prevalence of the Italian name bears out this judgement and illustrates the contribution of the Italian strain to the development of modern Argentina. The earlier immigrants, Lombards, Piedmontese, and Venetians, were mostly peasants, labourers and farmers, who moved inland to the agricultural colonies, raised sugar and tobacco in San Luis, and grew vines in Mendoza. The

---

[1] *International Migrations*, ii. 162.
[2] Op. cit., p. 193.
[3] M. G. and E. T. Mulhall, *Handbook of the River Plate* (5th edn., Buenos Aires, 1885), p. 14.

southerners flocked to the cities,[1] where in fact the bulk of Argentine immigrants have stayed. Indeed, even in the sixties, 'the golden era of Argentine colonization', in Jefferson's phrase,[2] only a sixth of all the immigrants entering Argentina settled on the land. Buenos Aires may properly be described as one of the greatest Italian cities in the world; and the concentration of immigrants in the cities has added to the excessive urbanization of Argentina (though this is characteristic of most Latin American countries) and to the lack of balance between Buenos Aires and its hinterland and the interior and southern provinces.

In Brazil, where the early Italian immigrants were also predominantly northerners,[3] it was mainly to the coffee fazendas of São Paulo—to live at little more than subsistence levels—and to the three southern states that the main stream flowed. In 1891 alone more than 130,000 Italians entered Brazil. More than half a million more came between 1894 and 1903. 'The labour on the great coffee estates of São Paulo', observed Lord Bryce, in 1912, 'is almost entirely Italian'; but, as Bryce also noted, in Rio Grande do Sul the Italians had become well-to-do peasant proprietors;[4] and while São Paulo and Santos are the chief 'Italian' cities of Brazil, the agricultural settlements in Rio Grande do Sul, which began in 1875, are the pride of the Italians of south Brazil.

The deliberate policy of Fascist Italy was primarily responsible for the rapid decline in Italian emigration to Argentina and Brazil in the late twenties; and nowhere else in Latin America did Italian migration ever attain to comparable proportions, though in Uruguay and Peru

[1] R. F. Foerster, *The Italian Emigration of our Times* (Harvard Univ. Press, 1924), pp. 266-7.
[2] Op. cit., p. 98.   [3] Foerster, op. cit., p. 309.
[4] James Bryce, *South America, Observations and Impressions* (New York, Macmillan, 1912), p. 406.

there are important and influential Italian communities. As for the less enterprising Spaniards, like the Portuguese, they shunned rural pursuits, and it is perhaps also the rankling memories of the wars of independence that made the Spanish in Argentina, except for the hard-working Basques, in general less acceptable than the Portuguese in Brazil, and less acceptable than the Italians. After Argentina, Cuba, the magnet of the immigrant in the Caribbean area, is the country they have entered in most numbers, and the flow there continued even after this last outpost of empire fell from Spanish hands.[1]

The chief contribution of Italy to the development of Latin America has been the labour of her sons, and in Argentina and Brazil Great Britain played a complementary role as a source of capital and technical skill. But the rivals of the Italians as immigrants were not the Spanish or the Portuguese or the English but, certainly in Brazil, the Germans; and throughout Latin America the Germans, though few in numbers, have exercised a greater influence than the bare statistics would suggest.

The largest, the most *reichsdeutsch*, the most compact, and the oldest German migration to Latin America has been to Brazil. Since 1818 Germans have entered Brazil in a thin but steady stream. Much reduced at the close of the nineteenth century, the movement gathered strength in the decade before the first World War, and again in the nineteen-twenties (22,168 in 1924). Yet less than a quarter of a million Germans have emigrated to Brazil, and, of these, more than one half represent a twentieth-century and, in a quite large part, a post-1918 migration. Even when to these German immigrants are added Austrians and others

---

[1] D. C. Corbitt, 'Immigration in Cuba', *Hispanic American Historical Review*, xxii (1942), pp. 280–308. Mexico has welcomed Spanish Republican refugees, but the Peninsular Spaniard is generally disliked.

claimed to be of German blood, the total is still not large,[1] and there has, moreover, been considerable re-emigration, both to other Latin American countries and back to Germany. The fact that there are in Brazil nearly a million people of German or part German stock is to be attributed to a high birth-rate among the immigrants rather than to large and continued reinforcements from the Fatherland.[2]

Yet south Brazil, under the stimulus of German colonization, has presented a highly successful example of pioneer settlement spread over a long period of time. It is to the three southern states of Rio Grande do Sul, Santa Catarina, and Paraná, and, later, to São Paulo, that German emigration has been principally directed. In São Paulo, where the coffee crop required the large estate and an ample labour supply, the agricultural settler, which is what the early immigrant was, and the small holder, had no place till recent times. But in the three southern states the great land-owners were from the first willing and indeed anxious to dispose of their property, either to immigrants or to land companies.[3] The first settlements took place in the eighteen twenties; and in Rio Grande do Sul, where they are most

[1] *Revista de Imigração e Colonização*, i, No. 4 (Oct. 1940); *International Migrations*, ii. 164.

[2] Cf. Hugo Grothe, *Die Deutschen in Übersee* (Berlin, Zentralverlag, 1932), pp. 34–7. For the literature on the Germans in Brazil see the bibliographies of R. Maack and A. Marchant in the *Handbook of Latin American Studies*, 1938 (ed. Lewis Hanke, Harvard Univ. Press, 1939). Maack, a German geographer, would have it that the people 'of German blood' in the three southern states of Rio Grande do Sul, Santa Catarina, and Paraná alone totalled 921,000 in 1939. 'The Germans of South Brazil: a German View', *Quarterly Journal of Inter-American Relations*, i (July, 1939), p. 9. Grothe's figure, in 1932, was 515,000 (op. cit., p. 45). The *Handwörterbuch des Grenz- und Ausland-Deutschtums* (Band 1, Lieferung 7, Breslau, 1935), p. 516, gives the total 'German-speaking' population of Brazil in 1935 as between 800,000 and 850,000. Other estimates put the population of German stock at a million and a quarter.

[3] R. Paula Lopes, 'Land Settlement in Brazil', *International Labour Review*, xxxiii (1936), pp. 170–1.

numerous, the Germans, until the arrival of the Italians in the eighteen-seventies, were almost the only colonists, advancing, after a hard beginning, from the neighbourhood of the Jacuí river (one of the most compact areas of German settlement in Brazil) to the hills and forests of the northern and north-western parts of the state. In Santa Catarina, where the first settlement took place in 1829, intensive colonization began after 1848, when Dr. Hermann Blumenau undertook to open up the region of the Itajaí river and the Hamburger Colonisationsverein began its labours; and Blumenau is now the centre of one of the most completely German districts in Brazil. Nearly the whole population has blue eyes and fair hair. Paraná, where the most important German centre is Curitiba, has received fewer immigrants, but in Paraná also the German colonist has been a transforming influence. The fact that southern Brazil has been a true zone of expanding settlement is due to the Germans, later joined by other immigrants.

Three ships left the port of Hamburg in the mid-nineteenth century. One sailed to New Orleans and its passengers proceeded up the Mississippi to Missouri. After a hundred years their descendants had merely a sentimental interest in their origin. A second sailed for Rio de Janeiro and its passengers went to southern Brazil. Their descendants 'speak German, think German and vote German'. It is tempting to conclude that the Anglo-Saxons could, while the Portuguese could not, absorb the new-comers. But the third ship sailed for Adelaide, and the descendants of its passengers have retained their German individuality with a far greater tenacity than their Missouri compatriots in an environment yet more thoroughly Anglo-Saxon.[1]

The reasons why the Germans in the agricultural com-

[1] M. L. Hansen, *The Immigrant in American History* (Harvard Univ. Press, 1940), pp. 24–5.

munities of southern Brazil have retained to a high degree their sense of German nationality while the Germans in the United States have not, are not, indeed, to be found in the superior assimilative qualities of the Anglo-Saxon race, nor even in the reluctance of the Germans in Brazil to submit to assimilation. They lie rather in the historical conditions of settlement and in the isolation in which these communities have lived. In most of the Latin American countries the German immigrant has shown a remarkable adaptability, and has identified himself closely with the political, economic, and social life of the country of his adoption. But in Brazil the German colonists were concentrated in remote and thinly peopled areas, distant from the seats of government. They were left to organize their own economic, social, and educational life. Pioneers on the frontier, they clung, as the Germans in Missouri and Texas also clung, to old and familiar ways. But in the United States the onward sweep of the frontier did not admit of the perpetuation of foreign enclaves within the nation. In Brazil the conditions of settlement did. The German colonists were aliens in a land which welcomed but hardly cherished them. Was it surprising that they should have begun to create a new Germany in the heart of southern Brazil?

Yet even before the advent of the National-Socialist State in Germany there were repeated complaints that the Germans in Brazil were in fact becoming Brazilians, and when that state arrived, the German communities in Brazil were at once subjected to the full force of National-Socialist propaganda, as they had earlier been subjected to the doctrines of Pan-Germanism. The complete panoply of National-Socialist organizations appeared, and German political and German economic penetration now proceeded hand in hand. Nor is there any doubt that the Third Reich recruited in Brazil a dangerous subversive element, particularly among the later immigrants. Yet the degree of success which this propaganda obtained must still remain a matter of debate. The traditions of the Germans in Brazil have been those of an industrious, law-abiding, and prosperous element in the nation. They were, and still are, widely regarded as model colonists. Some at least are more Brazilian than German. Whatever their sympathies, German-Brazilians of the second and third generation realized that their future lay in Brazil, and in 1942–5, as in 1917–18, the mass of the German communities remained quiescent. Nevertheless the dangers inherent in this situation were not lost on the Brazilian Government.[1] Since 1937 the authorities have prosecuted an energetic campaign designed to break down the physical and intellectual barriers still surrounding the German-Brazilians, and this campaign was intensified after Brazil declared war on Germany in August 1942. The Germans in Brazil face the choice earlier faced by the Germans in the United States; but 'because', in the words of Edmund Burke, 'half a dozen grasshoppers under a fern make the field ring with their importunate chink, whilst thousands of great cattle . . . chew the cud and are silent, pray do not imagine that those who make the noise are the only inhabitants of the field'.[2]

After Brazil the largest German emigration to Latin America has been to Argentina. But not only was German emigration to Argentina less extensive and less *reichsdeutsch* than the movement to Brazil; it was less distinctively agricultural. In the whole history of Argentine immigration up to 1941 only some 153,000 Germans entered the

[1] See B. W. Diffie, 'Some Foreign Influences in Contemporary Brazilian Politics', *Hispanic American Historical Review*, xx (1940), pp. 402–29.

[2] This is also Dr. J. A. Hawgood's view of the Germans in the United States. *The Tragedy of German-America* (New York and London, Putnam's, 1940), p. 308.

country, and even of these a considerable proportion came between 1918 and 1930, while of the pre-1924 immigrants about one half are known to have re-emigrated.[1] Before 1924, moreover, German immigration was exceeded by Russian, predominantly German-Russian, and it was exceeded on balance by Austro-Hungarian. The German-speaking population of Argentina is thus varied in origin and divided by strongly marked characteristics. As in Brazil the earlier settlers, Germans and German-speaking Swiss, were agriculturists, and Jefferson has noted how the children of the German settlers in the Santa Fe colony of Esperanza called themselves Germans, a thing practically unknown among the Italians and French.[2] The later immigrants belonged primarily to the professional, commercial, and artisan classes, though the newer and best-organized agricultural colonies in Misiones are German. But even German sources do not place the German-speaking population of Argentina at more than a quarter of a million, mostly settled in the three provinces of Buenos Aires, Santa Fe, and Entre Ríos, in the Territory of Misiones, and in Buenos Aires itself.[3]

These Argentine Germans were too few, in comparison with the Italians, to count for much in the economic development of the country. But the importance of those organizations in which Germans traditionally love to associate, and of the great German commercial, shipping, and banking houses as an instrument of National-Socialist penetration, was readily appreciated by the Third Reich, and the Argentine-Germans, like the Brazilian-Germans, felt, after 1933, the full impact of National-Socialist regi-

[1] *Revista de Economía Argentina,* xliii (1944), pp. 61–2; Grothe, op. cit., p. 16. [2] Op. cit., p. 68.

[3] From a report of Dr. W. Lütge, the Director of the Deutschen Volksbundes für Argentinien, quoted in the *Berliner Tageblatt,* 10 Aug. 1938. Cf. Grothe, op. cit., p. 20.

mentation. Already in 1938 there were disturbing accounts of German schools in which the Spanish language was unknown and National-Socialist doctrines were upheld, and in a series of reports issued in 1941 and 1942 a Committee of the Argentine Chamber of Deputies, established to investigate 'anti-Argentine activities', produced detailed evidence of the extraordinary ramifications of National-Socialist organizations among the Germans in Argentina and of the wide range of their activities. Nor, it must be added, were these activities viewed altogether without sympathy on the 'extremist fringe' of Argentine politics.

In one other South American country outside the 'pioneer hinterland', European immigration, though small in scale, has played an influential part. Chile has never been an immigration country in the sense of Argentina and Brazil; it never can become such; but south-central Chile has absorbed a considerable immigration, and in this immigration also German colonists have played a distinctive part. The movement, as in southern Brazil, was a movement of pioneers, of small farmers and peasants who came to find new homes in unknown lands. Valdivia, when the first Germans came there between 1846 and 1850, 'was not Chile, but Chilean territory'. It consisted of 'great expanses of impassable forest in which were scattered occasional grassy, open plains'; and when the German colony was established on Lake Llanquihue in 1853 the road from Puerto Montt 'had to be cut out with the axe, step by step. It took several months to traverse the twelve miles.' 'The woods were so wet they would not burn at all; the ground was a veritable sponge into which one sank at every step.'[1] This colonization was complete by 1861. It was followed, in the eighteen-eighties, by that of the

[1] Mark Jefferson, *Recent Colonisation in Chile* (New York, American Geographical Society, Research Series, No. 6, 1921), pp. 17–18 and 24–5.

frontera, as the frontier region south of the Bío-Bío and north of Valdivia, long the refuge of the Araucanian Indians, is called, and settlements have also been attempted in southern Patagonia, the last of the undeveloped territory of Chile, and on the island of Chiloé, where man wages a losing battle with the forest.

But immigration to Chile has been small. The *frontera* was colonized by some 36,000 immigrants, German, Swiss, English, French, and Spanish, as well as Chileans. Yet the *frontera* absorbed ten times as many immigrants as did Valdivia. As for the 'Germanization of Southern Chile', it is, Mark Jefferson has written, 'simply a myth'. 'There is no town or settlement in the country where a majority of the people are of German origin or speak German.'[1] The census of 1930, indeed, recorded the presence of less than 13,000 Germans, Austrians, and Swiss in the whole of the country, and apart from the influx of German-Jewish refugees between 1937 and 1941, it is improbable that the German element in the population of Chile amounts to much more than 30,000.[2] Nevertheless, in Valdivia at least, the Germans, though outnumbered by Chileans, remain the dominating influence. 'Whether in the cities or on the farms, foreigners are in command',[3] and like the Germans in south Brazil these Chilean-Germans have proved themselves a transforming influence in the life of the country in which they have settled.

Elsewhere in Latin America, except in Cuba, European immigration has been numerically insignificant, but not necessarily, therefore, uninfluential. The Italians in Peru have enjoyed an influence out of all proportion to their

---

[1] Ibid., pp. 8, 28, 35.
[2] Cf. *Handwörterbuch des Grenz- und Ausland-Deutschtums* (Band ii, Lieferung i, Breslau, 1936), p. 18.
[3] McBride, *Chile: Land and Society*, p. 298.

numbers. So also have small groups of Germans, ranging from some 3,000 in Bolivia to some 16,000 in Mexico, who, by their skills and enterprise, their careful cultivation of the surrounding peoples, and their easy adaptation to a new environment, secured for themselves a firm footing. In Colombia, Ecuador, Peru, and Bolivia, as well as in Brazil, Germans were the pioneers of civil aviation. They owned and operated large coffee-plantations in Central America; they trained armies and established schools; and here and there, as in Paraguay, they established small agricultural colonies.

Paris was the intellectual capital of Latin America in the nineteenth century as London was the financial capital. But in the peopling of the continent Britain and France have played a minor part. French immigrants indeed exceeded German in Argentina, and English, Scottish, and Irish names are fairly common both in Argentina and Chile.[1] But the influence of Great Britain and France was not primarily exerted through the immigrant. In Paraguay the almost forgotten name of Nueva Australia recalls an episode in Australian history, and Brazil, like Mexico, received, after the civil war in the United States, its quota of confederate exiles. In Argentina the Jewish Colonization Society has sought since 1891 to establish Jews on the land and has demonstrated that, in favourable conditions, the urban Jew can change his mode of life.[2] Syrians (mostly Lebanese Christians) and Palestinian Arabs are, under the popular denomination of 'Turks', scattered from one end of the continent to the other, and their proclivity for retail trade and huckstering has not added to their popularity.

[1] According to Argentine statistics French emigration to Argentina between 1857 and 1941 totalled 239,250 and British 75,650.

[2] For the remarkable work of the ICA colonies see E. Schwarz and J. C. Te Velde, 'Jewish Agricultural Settlement in Argentina: The ICA Experiment', *Hispanic American Historical Review*, xix (1939), pp. 185–203.

Finally, Poles (mostly in Argentina and Brazil), Russians, Rumanians, Yugoslavs, have added to the immigrant stream. For like the United States, Latin America has had its 'older' and its 'newer' immigration, the newer being the increase in the migration of eastern European peoples and the arrival of Japanese. Thus, both in Argentina and Brazil a decline in Latin immigration and an increased arrival of eastern Europeans were strongly marked in the nineteen-twenties,[1] and were accompanied in Brazil by a new phenomenon, the rapid influx of Japanese.

The days were, under Spanish rule, when the Manila galleon brought the silks of China to Acapulco and Mexico, and oriental wares filled the shops of Lima. But already in the eighteenth century the Philippine trade was in decline. For a time, in the nineteenth century, the American clipper ships, touching at South American ports, *en route* for China, kept the trade routes open. But, isolated as they were behind their mountain barriers, even the west coast states of South America looked eastwards across the Atlantic rather than westwards across the Pacific. The demand for labour on the guano islands of Peru and the sugar-plantations of Cuba led, between 1847 and 1874, to the organization of the Chinese coolie traffic, and in those years more than 74,000 coolies were brought to Peru, many to be openly sold into slavery. More than 114,000 were sent to Cuba between 1847 and 1867. This was the origin of the comparatively substantial Chinese populations of those two countries, and in Cuba another 150,000 Chinese were admitted in the present century.[2] But Latin

[1] 'Immigration and Settlement in Brazil, Argentina, and Uruguay', *International Labour Review*, xxxv (1937), pp. 217–18; *Revista de Economía Argentina*, xliii (1944), p. 62.

[2] Anita Bradley, *Trans-Pacific Relations of Latin America* (New York, Institute of Pacific Relations, 1941), pp. 49–53; Corbitt, op. cit., *Hispanic American Historical Review*, xxii (1942), p. 307. There is a substantial Chinese

American interest in China and Japan was almost negligible in the nineteenth century, and it was not till the close of that century that there were signs of an awakening Japanese interest in Latin America.

These signs were the establishment of diplomatic relations between Japan and Peru in 1873, the negotiation of commercial treaties with various Latin American states, beginning with Mexico in 1888, the dispatch of Japanese labourers to Peru in 1898, and the first Japanese settlement in Brazil in 1908. In Peru the Japanese community now numbers between 20,000 and 30,000 people, is mostly engaged in retail trade and small crafts and industries, lives in and about the capital city of Lima and the port of Callao, and owns most of the barbers' shops, though there are also agricultural colonies in the cotton-growing valleys of the coasts, particularly in the Chancay valley. Brazil, however, has been the chief focus of Japanese interest in Latin America, and in Brazil Japanese immigration has been a movement of capital as well as of people. It first became highly organized with the foundation of the Kaigai Kogyo Kabushiki Kaisha (Overseas Development Company) in 1917, but it was not till after the passage of the so-called exclusion act in the United States, in 1924, that it attained to high proportions. According to Japanese figures, there were less than 34,000 Japanese residents in Brazil in 1920; there were nearly 175,000 in 1934; and in 1943 the Japanese community in Brazil probably numbered between 200,000 and 250,000.[1]

The majority of these Japanese immigrants are agricultural settlers or labourers, carefully selected and trained in

community in Mexico, and Chinese are also scattered throughout Central America.

[1] J. F. Normano and Antonello Gerbi, *The Japanese in South America* (New York, John Day, 1943), pp. 12 and 36.

Japan. They live in the state of São Paulo (where they account for nearly a third of the agricultural production),[1] and they have distinguished themselves in the cultivation of cotton, sugar, rice, tea, and silk—this last an industry which they created. They have spread also into the states of Minas Gerais, Mato Grosso, and Paraná, and the Japanese also turned their attention to the acquisition of concessions in the states of Amazonas and Pará. Excellent and hard-working colonists, they have made a genuine contribution to Brazilian economic development. But they have also retained to a high degree their old loyalties and allegiances; they submitted to a rigorous control through institutions operated from Japan; and they finally succeeded in arousing the apprehensions of the Brazilian authorities not only on the grounds of their possible effect on the future composition of the Brazilian population but on those of political unreliability.

Japanese agricultural colonies have also been established in Colombia and Paraguay; but everywhere in Latin America the Japanese present a formidable problem of assimilation. They compete, on cheap terms, with native labour and native traders, and, like the Chinese, they have increasingly faced discrimination in the newer immigration and labour laws. In Peru, where, as in California, they have aroused unconcealed dislike, anti-Japanese riots have occurred, and an immigration law in 1936 was plainly directed against the Japanese 'invasion'. In Brazil the increase in Japanese immigration was partly responsible for the adoption of a quota system. Japan is no longer likely to find in Latin America an outlet for her surplus population.

Despite the variety in the composition of this immigrant stream to Latin America, the total number of immigrants arriving in the last hundred and twenty-five years cannot

[1] Ibid., p. 39.

exceed twelve million. This is not much more than a third of the total emigration to the United States between 1820 and 1940. A quite high proportion of these immigrants, moreover, were not permanent settlers, and the majority of them went to two countries, Argentina and Brazil. Yet, in the nineteen-thirties, under the shadow of the world depression, Latin America once again entered upon an era of immigration restriction. Argentina departed from its previous policy of the 'open door' and imposed severe limitations on immigration, which reached their height in 1938. Brazil adopted a quota system in 1934, and the Constitution of 1937 repeated a provision that immigration from any country should not exceed in any one year 2 per cent. of the total number of immigrants of that nationality who had settled in Brazil during the last fifty years. It was further decreed in 1938 that 80 per cent. of permanent approved immigrants must be agricultural workers. Uruguay, in 1932, forbade the entry of all except skilled workers under contract and not likely to compete with native labour. One after another, moreover, the Latin American countries enacted anti-alien employment laws, limiting the number of foreigners who might be employed in industrial or commercial enterprises.

The purpose of this legislation was to restrict the entry of wage-paid workers rather than of agricultural immigrants, for these, in theory, were still welcome. It was, in part, the result of agricultural and industrial unemployment, and of a desire to protect local labour markets. In part it reflected the new 'nationalism' in Latin America, concern at the changing composition of the immigrant stream, and concern also, towards the end of the decade, at the entry of the impecunious refugee. Exceptions from these limitations were sometimes made, in favour of Portuguese in Brazil, Basques in Argentina, Spanish republican refugees in Mexico, and the small Jewish settlement scheme in the Dominican Republic. But in general the policy of the Latin American countries since the early nineteen-thirties has been consistently restrictive, and it must be added that, despite a recommendation of the Inter-American Conference at Lima in 1938, that there should be no discrimination in Latin America against immigrants on ground of nationality, creed, or race, it has had a distinct anti-Jewish tinge.[1]

These restrictive and controlling tendencies may be relaxed. Though the population of Brazil has risen by more than 20 millions since 1900 and that of Argentina by 10 millions since the second census of 1895, these countries are still sparsely populated by comparison with Europe or the United States. Brazil still has an 'enormous area of undeveloped land of great fertility, situated in zones in which the European can easily become acclimatized'.[2] Argentina could certainly sustain a far greater population than at present, though under the present agrarian structure there is little room for the poor immigrant on the famous pampa, which contains 90 per cent. of the cultivated land. He must turn rather to the northern subtropical territories of Chaco, Formosa, and Misiones, where new colonies have been established in quite recent years, or to the limited possibilities afforded by the river valleys of Patagonia. The gradual breaking up of the great estates, however, the growth of industrialization, and the changing balance of social, economic, and political forces may well stimulate a fresh demand for immigrant labour, and many Argentines, in fact, believe that the present

[1] See E. W. H. Lumsden, 'Immigration and Politics in Latin America,' *Inter-American Quarterly*, ii. (Oct. 1940), pp. 64–73. For the Sosúa settlement scheme in the Dominican Republic see *Refugee Settlement in the Dominican Republic* (Washington, Brookings Institution, 1942).

[2] 'Immigration and Settlement in Brazil, Argentina, and Uruguay', *International Labour Review*, xxxv (1937), p. 225. *Ante*, pp. 7–8.

restrictions on immigration into their country must be revised. In Brazil the Government is anxious to develop and populate the interior as well as to advance industrial expansion at a fairly rapid rate, and the need for a more generous, though selective, immigration policy, if the country is to realize its vast potentialities, has been a constant theme of discussion.

Of the other Latin American republics, Bolivia has land in plenty, in its south-eastern lowlands, where the natural conditions are suitable both for agriculture and stock-raising,[1] and without a substantial increase in population the country faces a precarious future only too likely to repeat a tragic past. Colombia and Venezuela have been barely touched by immigration, and neither offers high inducements to the immigrant. In Colombia the opportunities for agricultural settlement are limited. Venezuela's need is great, but the European migrant, more likely to be welcomed in the tropical than the temperate areas, faces a cost of living extravagantly high and conditions more easily borne by the coloured than the white settler. Ecuador and Peru have their eastern valleys. But the development of these is not possible till the demand for tropical products is far greater than at present,[2] and nowhere else do the present conditions of landownership and of labour offer opportunities to other than wealthy migrants. In Chile the fertile Central Valley is populated to saturation under present conditions of land exploitation. Northern Chile is a barren desert, and the old southern frontier is no longer a major population outlet.[3] Nor are conditions much more favourable in Mexico and Central America. Mexico is a poor, not a rich, country. Seventy per cent. of its popula-

---

[1] *Ante*, p. 8.   [2] *Ante*, pp. 4–5.
[3] Bowman, *The Pioneer Fringe*, pp. 309–10; and *Limits of Land Settlement*, p. 303.

tion is engaged in agriculture, living at a subsistence level; yet fully a half of the national territory is incapable of agricultural exploitation, and even the crop land requires extensive irrigation. Mexico has been an emigration rather than an immigration country.[1] As for Central America, cheap native labour is there abundant, and such opportunities as are available to the immigrant are only in the most backward areas and under the most primitive conditions.

Latin America is widely regarded as one of the few areas left in the world capable of offering opportunities for settlement on any considerable scale. It may be so; but the movement of men is dependent on the movement of capital, on the provision of markets, and on the means devised to integrate the immigrant into a new and often alien economic and social structure; and the majority of the Latin American states cannot of their own resources provide the conditions and facilities which the immigrant requires. Nor should it be forgotten that the immigrant is apt to compete with vested interests and to dislocate established habit. Around him there is a clash of interests as well as of ideas; and it is in response to that clash that anti-immigrant sentiment has grown. It is obvious that immigration would, in the long run, assist the Latin American countries in the process of social and economic change which they are now undergoing. But it is in part dependent on that change; and, finally, it is clear, that so far as the immediate future is concerned, the emphasis will remain on the selected, the trained, and the assimilable immigrant. There is no sign that mass and indiscriminate immigration will again revive. The immigration frontiers of the world, like its other frontiers, are at present shrinking, not expanding frontiers.

[1] Between 1920 and 1929 alone net emigration to the United States amounted to more than 428,000. *International Migrations*, ii. 590.

IV

DEMOCRACY AND DICTATORSHIP

FROM the revolutionary wars the Spanish American
states emerged weak and exhausted. Their peoples had
passed from tutelage to independence. But they had yet
to comprehend and organize the freedom they had won.
They had achieved statehood but not nationhood, and for
self-government they were ill equipped. 'We are still too
little elevated from servitude', wrote Bolívar, 'to rise easily
to the proper enjoyment of liberty.'[1] The masses, oppressed
by poverty and ignorance, were indolent, docile and savage
by turns, and almost entirely illiterate, and for them
independence meant a change of masters not of systems.
The new ruling minority, the creole aristocracy of landowners and lawyers, was undisciplined and untrained; it
was, as Bolívar observed, 'without practice in public affairs'.
There was no organized public opinion and no middle class
to give stability to politics. For fifteen years the exercise of
authority had been fitful and violent; and the wars of
independence had encouraged the military not the political
virtues. The new states, moreover, or many of them, were
huge, and the problems of their administration complex.
Their centres of population were remote from one another
and the means of communication slow and hazardous.
Regional rivalries divided them. Local chieftains competed
for power. The brave new world which idealists wished to
build was contradicted by the facts of the political and
social order. Nations cannot be founded on political theory.

[1] 'Nosotros estábamos en un grado todavía más abajo de la servidumbre, y
por lo mismo con más dificultad para elevarnos al goce de la libertad.'
Vicente Lecuna, ed., *Cartas del Libertador* (10 vols., Caracas, Lit. y Tip. del
Comercio, 1929–30), i. 190; Belaunde, *Bolívar and the Political Thought of the
Spanish American Revolution,* p. 161.

Yet political theory ruled. The machinery of constitutional government has always exercised a peculiar fascination in Latin America.[1] Nowhere are constitutions more elaborate—or less observed; and the founders of the Spanish American republics attempted to establish a pattern of freedom in charters which combined the Declaration of the Rights of Man with the machinery of the Constitution of the United States. The American Constitution was the great exemplar of liberty. But it was the letter and the form of the Constitution rather than its spirit which so strongly appealed to its Latin American imitators. In the United States the fathers of the Constitution were concerned not to make America safe for democracy but to make democracy safe for America. Power was limited and divided, checked and balanced. The controlling principle was the rule of law; and the Constitution was itself the expression of a great moral and legal tradition, deeply rooted in seventeenth-century political thought and eighteenth-century colonial experience. These roots were lacking in Spanish America. The Spaniards are a highly individualistic people. The dignity of the individual is with them a passionate belief. This sense of personal dignity was as true of the Spaniard in America as of the Spaniard in Spain; but it was combined with the traditions in government of a paternal autocracy and a centralized absolutism; and the absolutism which Spanish constitutional theory predicated of the Crown, French revolutionary doctrine predicated of the people. While, therefore, the form of the American Constitution was in any event ill adapted to the needs of the new states, except perhaps in Argentina, and to the capacities of their peoples, French revolutionary thought

[1] See the interesting article of Kingsley Davis, 'Political Ambivalence in Latin America', *Journal of Legal and Political Sociology* (New York), i (1942), pp. 127–50.

triumphed over American constitutional theory. The Latin American dictator was the natural and inevitable product.

The contrast between form and reality, between logic and life, between theory and experience, could hardly have been more complete. 'The codes consulted by our law-givers', wrote Bolívar in 1812, 'were not such as could instruct them in the practical science of government, but rather the inventions of well-meaning visionaries, who, thinking in terms of ideal republics, sought to attain political perfection on the supposition of the perfectibility of the human race.'[1] 'Until our compatriots', he observed, in his famous Jamaica letter in 1815, 'acquire the political talents and virtues which distinguish our brothers of the north, entirely popular systems, far from being beneficial, will, I very much fear, come to be our ruin.' 'Is it conceiv-able', he asked, 'that a people but recently freed from its chains can ascend into the sphere of liberty without melting its wings like Icarus and plunging into the abyss?' The states of Spanish America, he believed, were not yet suited to 'perfectly representative institutions'; they needed 'the kindly guardianship of paternal governments' which would heal 'the sores and wounds of despotism and war'.[2]

There can be no question but that Bolívar was right. History and experience alike supported him, and, like John Adams and Alexander Hamilton, Bolívar perceived that democracy is not necessarily synonymous with liberty. Of the unfettered exercise of the popular will he entertained a profound distrust. It is, he affirmed in 1820, in words which John Adams himself might have written, 'a recognized principle in politics that a completely democratic govern-ment is as tyrannical as a despot. Thus, only a tempered

---

[1] Lecuna, op. cit., i. 36–7.　　　　[2] Ibid., i. 195–7.

government can be free.'[1] This was the explanation of his ardent and freely expressed admiration for English institutions and practice, and of his feeling, which San Martín also shared, for the principle of the rule of law. The judicial power, he remarked, in drafting his Constitution for Bolivia in 1826, 'is the measure of the welfare of the citizens; if there is liberty, if there is justice, they are made effective by this power. At times, the political organization has little importance, provided that the civil organization is perfect, if the laws are rigidly enforced and considered as inexorable as destiny.'[2]

San Martín's solution of this political problem was monarchy; and it may well be argued that the survival of the monarchy in Brazil was at least in part the explanation of Brazil's peaceful constitutional evolution in the nineteenth century. There was no abrupt break with the colonial past, no long struggle for the control of the instruments of government, no 'anarchistic equalitarianism'.[3] The Constitution of 1824, which survived for sixty-five years, recognized facts, if it ignored ideals[4]—some ideals. But Brazil was a fortunate exception. There the monarchy was of native growth. It was consolidated without long and bitter wars. It possessed, from the first, trained administrators, and it was peculiarly happy in the character of the second emperor, Dom Pedro. But, as Bolívar realized, what was possible in Brazil was not feasible elsewhere.

[1] Ibid., ii. 178; Belaunde, op. cit., p. 180. See also his Address to the Congress of Angostura in D. F. O'Leary, *Bolívar y la Emancipación de Sur-América. Memorias del General O'Leary* (2 vols., Madrid, Biblioteca Ayacucho, [n.d.]) i. 588–616.

[2] O'Leary, op. cit., ii. 531; Belaunde, op. cit., p. 252.

[3] A. K. Manchester, 'Constitutional Dictatorship in Brazil', in *South American Dictators during the First Century of Independence*, ed. A. C. Wilgus (Washington, D.C., George Washington Univ. Press, 1937), p. 430.

[4] M. W. Williams, *Dom Pedro the Magnanimous, Second Emperor of Brazil* (Chapel Hill, Univ. of North Carolina Press, 1937), p. 128.

The argument against the establishment of monarchical régimes was not that they would have meant 'a hierarchy of churchmen, landlords, mine owners, and wealthy merchants, with a following of lawyers, physicians, army officers, and the like'.[1] For this, in point of fact, is very much what nineteenth-century society in most of the Latin American countries tended to be. Nor was it that there were no possible candidates who might have been tempted to aspire to New World thrones. But a monarch imported from abroad, or a monarch elevated at home, could not have survived. Maximilian of Mexico was to be the tragic example of the first, Iturbide of the second. Haiti is the only other Latin American country to have established monarchs, but their fate can hardly be called happy, or their example inspiring.

Monarchy, then, was rejected, though it had many adherents and there were long and intricate negotiations now with this scion of a royal house and now with that. But rejected also were Bolívar's elaborate attempts to secure what was in fact a constitutional monarchy in disguise; and with anguish and despair the greatest of the Latin American dictators, nearing his tragic end, watched the spectre of anarchy rising from the ruins of empire. 'There is no faith in America,' he wrote in 1829, 'neither between men nor between nations. Treaties are only papers; constitutions, books; elections, combats; liberty, anarchy; and life, a torment.'[2]

In parts of Latin America, indeed, society itself seemed on the point of dissolution. In Argentina, in the eighteen-twenties, the national government disappeared. In 1820, the 'year of anarchy', the Province of Buenos Aires alone

---

[1] J. F. Rippy in Wilgus, op. cit., p. 19.
[2] Belaunde, op. cit., p. 377. See also the famous letter to General Flores. Lecuna, op. cit., ix. 376.

had at the least twenty-four governors. Local government fell into the hands of local caudillos, the gauchos, whom it took a gaucho, Rosas, to subdue. The nineteenth and the twelfth centuries, wrote Sarmiento, dwelt side by side, one inside the cities, the other outside them.[1]

'All interests, all ideas, all passions, met together to create agitation and tumult. Here was a chief who would have nought to do with the rest of the Republic; there, a community whose only desire was to emerge from its isolation; yonder, a government engaged in bringing Europe over to America; elsewhere, another to which the very name of civilization was odious; the Holy Tribunal of the Inquisition was reviving in some places; in others, liberty of conscience was proclaimed the first of human rights; the cry of one party was for confederation; of others for a central government; while each different combination was backed by strong and unconquerable passions.'[2]

Buenos Aires alone retained a certain degree of stability, which it owed principally to Rivadavia, and promised, in 1824, to form the nucleus of an ordered state; but not only did Argentina make war against Brazil, the provinces made war against Buenos Aires and one another; and the natural and inevitable opposition between Buenos Aires and the provinces—the one the proud city dominating the life and commerce of the republic, the others, jealous of its power and scornful of its manners, and strongly imbued with the sense of local independence—was long to give meaning and form to Argentine history.

Across the River Plate, conditions in the Banda Oriental of Uruguay, long coveted both by Argentina and Brazil, were equally chaotic. If ever a state was born of war and international rivalries, that state was Uruguay; and of its life after independence was achieved the Uruguayan

[1] *Life in the Argentine Republic*, p. 42.   [2] Ibid., p. 113.

historian, Zum Felde, has remarked: 'The leaders could readily agree on a general principle and declare: Nothing must separate us. And promptly they would be separated.'[1] Chile, it is true, attained to relative order by 1830, after having lived under five constitutions in twelve years, and Paraguay, under the iron despotism of Dr. Francia, enjoyed peace, if little else, for more than a quarter of a century of almost complete isolation from the outside world. But Bolivia, after an attempt to subjugate Peru, was engulfed in anarchy, and the political heirs of Great Colombia seemed set on a course to justify Bolívar's despairing words: 'I believe all lost for ever and the country and my friends submerged in a tempest of calamities.'[2] Nor in Mexico and Central America was the prospect much brighter. As constitutions followed constitutions and presidents followed presidents in bewildering succession, the Spanish American states, rent by factional and regional strife, seemed destined to move, in monotonous rhythm, from an excess of anarchy to an excess of despotism.

Dictatorship was inevitable, even necessary. The conditions of life, physical and economic, the essentially hierarchic structure of society, its racial composition, its traditions, were alike inimical to the working of representative institutions. Three centuries of colonial experience were not to be obliterated by twenty-five years of revolutionary dogmatism. From one point of view, indeed, the dictators who so early arose were as much the expression of the Spanish American revolutions as Napoleon was an expression of the French Revolution. From another, dictatorship represented the triumph of experience over theory. It was the tradition of personal rule that survived, reinforced by that Praetorianism which was the inevitable

---

[1] Quoted by L. W. Bealer in Wilgus, op. cit., p. 121.
[2] Belaunde, op. cit., p. 397.

legacy of the revolutionary wars. The army was the immediate, if not the ultimate, support of the ruling faction of the governing oligarchy or of the dictator which replaced it; and though it is, apparently, colonels and majors, rather than generals, who now make revolutions, the tradition of barrack-room intervention in politics dies hard. Nor was it difficult to legalize despotism. Even where constitutional forms were observed, the Constitution tended to make the President strong, and circumstances to make him stronger. Where, as in most Spanish American countries, dictators, at one time or another, assumed the 'sum of power', it needed only a little manipulation to establish their legal authority or a plausible and easily found excuse to pose, with Messianic fervour, as the restorers of the laws and the Constitution.

All the Spanish American states, without exception, have experienced periods of violence and tyranny, some of prolonged violence and prolonged tyranny. Rosas ruled Argentina for twenty-three years before he was overthrown to die in exile near Southampton. Francia's 'reign of terror' in Paraguay endured for twenty-six years. Gómez was the master of Venezuela for twenty-seven years and Díaz of Mexico for thirty-four. It would be folly to assume that these absolutisms were wholly unpopular. Rosas, the greatest and the worst of the Argentine tyrants, ruled by terror, but he ruled also with the support of the rural masses. Francia's despotism was founded on the determination of the creoles of Asunción to preserve their independence against Buenos Aires and on the veneration which he inspired among the Guaraní and mestizo peasantry. Díaz enjoyed the support of the landowners, the Church, and the army, as well as a distinguished reputation abroad. Even Francisco Solano López, who, whatever interpretation may be placed upon the origins of the Paraguayan war, bears a fearful responsibility for that struggle, and led his people along a road of serfdom, blood, and tears, retained their loyalty to the hideous end,[1] and is not now without honour in his own country.

There were autocrats who waded through blood to presidential thrones, ignorant adventurers who perpetrated unspeakable crimes. But not all dictators were tyrants, for though, as Lord Acton has remarked, 'absolute power corrupts absolutely', there were relatively good as well as wholly bad dictators, and some, even among the worst, by breaking and moulding lesser despots to their will, helped to substitute a larger conception of the state as a nation for the agglomeration of personal and local loyalties which hindered its action and restrained its growth.[2] Nor is it possible to dismiss the history of a continent during a long period merely as the history of dictatorship tempered by assassination and revolution, to believe that all the protagonists in this drama were actuated 'by no other motive than a desire for self-aggrandizement, and their respective supporters by nothing save a desire for booty',[3] or to brush contemptuously aside the efforts of the Spanish American peoples to establish their liberties by written constitutions as *pálabras y nada más*.

For the Spanish Americans cherish their freedom. In Latin America persons have always mattered more than programmes, and parties were, and are, as much the expression of personal loyalties as of political principles. The dictators themselves were personal rulers; there was not,

[1] See P. H. Box, *The Origins of the Paraguayan War* (2 vols., Urbana, Illinois, Univ. of Illinois Studies in the Social Sciences, xv, Nos. 3 and 4 [1930]), a brilliant study by an English scholar too early lost to scholarship.

[2] Cf. C. H. Haring, *South American Progress* (Harvard Univ. Press, 1934), p. 15, much the best short analysis of modern South American history.

[3] The phrase of Cecil Jane, who does not believe it. *Liberty and Despotism in Spanish America*, p. 4.

and could not be, that regimentation which has been the foundation of the modern totalitarian state. It was an excess of individualism which, in the guise of a conflict between Centralists and Federalists, Clericals and Anti-clericals, Conservatives and Liberals, gave such bitterness to party strife and sundered the rivers of the republics' life. And beneath this turbulence, life followed its old and customary pattern. Politics was a way of life and of making a living remote from the control and interests of the masses. The majority were, and were content to be, spectators of events, indifferent to the form of government, provided government did not too arrogantly trespass on the affairs of the governed. Even revolutions, those established extra-legal habits of replacing one régime by another, were often parochial affairs.

'It is', wrote W. H. Hudson, in 1885, of one of the then most chaotic of Latin American countries, Uruguay, 'the perfect republic: the sense of emancipation experienced in it by the wanderer from the Old World is indescribably sweet and novel . . . the knot of ambitious rulers all striving to pluck each other down have no power to make the people miserable. The unwritten constitution, mightier than the written one, is in the heart of every man to make him still a republican and free with a freedom it would be hard to match anywhere else on the globe.'[1]

These general conditions obtained at one time or another in all the Spanish American republics, and in some the conventional pattern of politics is still little changed. Intentions may be good; but the forces of inertia are too strong, the struggle for power is too ardent, and the problem of administrative efficiency too great. Hence oligarchy gives place to dictatorship and dictatorship to revolution. But the differences in the political evolution of the Latin American states are at least as great as the resemblances,

---

[1] *The Purple Land* (Duckworth, 1904), pp. 334-5.

and far more significant. The basis of their future national differentiation already existed during the colonial period, in race, in custom, and in administration; and the Bourbon reforms in the eighteenth century themselves stimulated a regional self-consciousness and a local nationalism. Paradoxically, the territorial definition of the new states was already vaguely fixed before the wars of independence began. But the transition from statehood to nationhood, and all that that implies, was a longer and far more complex process than that from colony to republic; dictatorship was, apparently, and may still be, an essential element in it; but it followed different lines in different countries; it is still imperfectly understood; and it is not yet by any means complete. The so-called 'nationalist movements' in Latin America are born not of the assurance of national unity but of the absence of assurance.

In South America three states early established for themselves a position of marked superiority. Brazil, under the rule of her scholar-emperor, Pedro II, was, in her imperial form, her 'peculiar institution' of slavery, her generally peaceful internal evolution, *sui generis*, until, in 1889, a bloodless revolution deposed the emperor and prepared the way for the establishment of the Federal Republic. In Chile the reign of the caudillos virtually ceased with the adoption of the Constitution of 1833, and under the dominance of a landed, but not always enlightened, aristocracy, Chile evolved a relatively stable political order and a remarkable quasi-parliamentary system. Argentina's institutional organization was confirmed when, in 1861, the battle of Pavón, fought between the army of Buenos Aires and the forces of the Argentine Confederation, established in 1853, resulted in 'the definitive union of all the Argentine provinces';[1] it was finally consummated by the federaliza-

[1] Levene, *A History of Argentina*, p. 463.

tion of the city of Buenos Aires itself in 1880. In each of these countries the immigrant and immigrant capital were, in lesser or greater degree, transforming influences; in each, economic progress was accompanied by a widening of the basis of society and of politics, the rise of new social forces, a new industrial aristocracy, a middle class, and organized labour; and what wheat and meat were to Argentina, cotton and then coffee were to Brazil and nitrates and copper to Chile. Yet, in the face of the world economic crisis, each returned to violence as well as fraud in politics. Chile's political life was plunged into confusion. Brazil, which had abandoned monarchy for republic in 1889, abandoned constitutionalism for dictatorship in 1930. Argentina, whose politics had undergone a progressive liberalization since 1890, retrod a well-worn path in the nineteen-thirties and finally, in 1943, frankly exchanged the ballot-box for the barrack-room.

Three other countries, Colombia, Costa Rica, and Uruguay, emerged at the end of the nineteenth century from conditions of instability or dictatorship to develop democratic or quasi-democratic institutions, though only in Colombia has there been no interruption in this peaceful constitutional evolution. Here a devastating civil war, from 1899 to 1902, caused 'incalculable losses. On the battlefields 100,000 men or more perished; thousands were maimed for life; commerce was ruined.'[1] Colombia then, in 1903, suffered the loss of Panamá. Yet these were the last disasters to overtake the republic, and thenceforth its history was 'happily, not spectacular and only conspicuous for those qualities which need no record'.[2] On the whole,

[1] J. M. Henao and G. Arrubla, *History of Colombia* (trans. and ed. by J. F. Rippy, Chapel Hill, Univ. of North Carolina Press, 1938), p. 519.

[2] F. A. Kirkpatrick, *Latin America, a Brief History* (Cambridge Univ. Press, 1938), p. 262.

since the fall of the last dictator, who retired into voluntary exile in 1909, elections have been genuinely fought and peacefully won, and have resolved themselves into contests between Clerical Conservatives and mildly Anti-clerical Liberals, who, though much given to divisions between themselves, have held power since 1930, have severed the Church from the State, and have pursued a policy of moderate social reform; and, more, perhaps, than in most Latin American countries, the conflict of political parties represents a genuine conflict of political principles.

Costa Rica, with the advantages of a comparatively homogeneous population, a high degree of literacy, and a considerable number of small landowners, has also succeeded since 1902 (with a brief interval between 1917 and 1919) in solving its problems by constitutional methods, in notable contrast to its Central American neighbours. Indeed, so vigorous is political debate in this small nation-state that it may be argued that the average Costa Rican is, if anything, too politically minded. Finally, Uruguay, like Colombia and Costa Rica, dates its peaceful democratic development from the turn of the century. Of the twenty-five governments which ruled, or failed to rule, Uruguay between 1830 and 1903, 'nine were forced out of power, two were liquidated by assassination and one by grave injury, ten resisted successfully one or more revolutions, and three were free of serious disturbance'.[1] But since the first term of its great President, José Batlle y Ordóñez (1903–7), the republic has undergone a remarkable transformation. From one of the most backward of the South American countries it became, within a few years, one of the most vigorous and most progressive. As the state entered into business and industry, and embarked on a

[1] S. G. Hanson, *Utopia in Uruguay* (New York, Oxford Univ. Press, 1938), p. 3.

programme of state socialism and advanced labour legislation, Uruguay offered to the world the example of the first 'New Deal' in the Americas.

Uruguay's constitutional evolution, however, like that of Argentina, was interrupted in the nineteen-thirties, when President Terra, in 1933, dissolved Congress, carried out a *coup d'état*, convoked a Constituent Assembly, and secured a new Constitution. President Terra's excuse for this procedure was the need for decisive action in meeting the world economic depression, which struck Uruguay with great severity, and the inability, as he alleged, of the somewhat cumbersome constitutional machinery then existing to provide such action. But its result was deeply to divide Uruguay's two traditional political parties against themselves; and an arrangement in the new Constitution, which entitled the largest minority party not only to representation in the Senate but also in the Cabinet, placed a premium on political obstruction and in turn led to further extra-constitutional action in 1942 and fresh constitutional revision. To the observer from outside, Uruguayan politics are apt to exhibit a scene of extraordinary confusion, heightened by the polemics so freely indulged in by the press. But there can be no question of the attachment of the Uruguayan people to the processes of democratic government.

Chile, Colombia, Costa Rica, and Uruguay are the countries of Latin America which most nearly approach to the true type of representative democracy; and to this type Argentina until recently also conformed. They enjoy vigorous political debate; elections are something more than a formality; and the press is free. All four have attained to a relatively high degree of social coherence, and in them the transition from statehood to nationhood has definitely been achieved. Yet only Chile and Uruguay have benefited to any considerable extent by immigration, and only Costa Rica and Uruguay are predominantly peopled by a pure white strain. Geography as well as history has imposed a certain unity upon Chile, and Uruguay and Costa Rica are small and compact. But Colombia is one of the larger Latin American states and it is still under-populated. In Costa Rica the system of landholding has been favourable to the evolution of political democracy, but this is certainly not true of Chile; and while in Uruguay and Costa Rica there is a high degree of literacy, it is far less high in Chile and Colombia. Those who seek a common factor to explain a similar movement of civilization in different countries at the same time may, perhaps, find it in the growth, through economic diversification and industrialization, of a middle class; yet the economy of all of these countries, even including Chile, is still primarily an agrarian economy, and in none has diversification proceeded far.

The remaining states of Latin America all profess a common democratic faith; but this is the substance of things hoped for rather than the evidence of things already seen; and for some of the republics democracy, as a form of government, means little more than republicanism. Some, such as the Dominican Republic, El Salvador, Nicaragua, Honduras, and Guatemala, are dictatorships undisguised, or only lightly camouflaged, though in Guatemala, General Ubico, the dread and envy of his neighbours, who had ruled his country with an iron hand since 1931 and ruled it not unwell, was overthrown in 1944 by a 'democratic' movement. General Ubico described himself as a 'Liberal Progressive', and certainly had some claim—not shared by all his Central American colleagues—to the latter epithet. But the limits set by the social and economic structure of these countries, and by the low educational and cultural level of the politically inert masses, themselves define the form and quality of their governments. Even in Central America, however, dictators now prefer to prolong their power by 'constitutional' means, if possible,[1] through amendments to the Constitutions or by the staging of plebiscites.

Elsewhere in Latin America the outward forms of political democracy are somewhat more scrupulously preserved. Mexico, like Brazil, is in a class apart. The machinery of representative and responsible government there exists and to some extent functions, and political democracy in Mexico, limited and halting as it is, is not a meaningless phrase. Cuba, which held unprecedentedly free elections in 1944, operates, somewhat precariously, a semi-parliamentary system, and Venezuela, which endured, till the death of Gómez in 1935, one of the most oppressive dictatorships in Latin American history, has moved from absolute tyranny to relative freedom. Peru is to outward appearance a democracy, but the party with the greatest popular appeal, the Alianza Popular Revolucionaria Americana, was, till recently, banned from formal participation in politics, and the traditions of the ruling class are inimical as much to the theory of democratic government as to its practice.

Politics, indeed, in the Andean republics of Peru, Ecuador, and Bolivia, where the Indian masses are inert and apathetic and the bulk of the population is illiterate, are still the monopoly of a privileged minority; and behind the political disorder which has characterized Bolivia, Paraguay, and Ecuador, lie the solid facts of ignorance and poverty and of social and economic incoherence. Paraguay has barely recovered from her devastating war (1865–70) with Brazil, Uruguay, and Argentina, in which two-thirds

[1] R. H. Fitzgibbon, ' "Continuismo" in Central America and the Caribbean', *Inter-American Quarterly*, ii (July 1940), pp. 56–74.

of her people perished, and still less from her conflict with Bolivia (1932–5); and the tragic sequence of politics in Bolivia is heightened by the sense of bitterness and national frustration of a country which lost in one war its Pacific coastline to Chile and failed in a second to secure an outlet to the Atlantic from Paraguay.

There is no sealed pattern of democracy. If democracy means merely a particular form of representative government, then, in Latin America as a whole, it is an aspiration rather than a fact, and not everywhere an aspiration. But the conventional distinction between a democracy and a dictatorship is no sufficient criterion by which to judge the working of government in the Latin American states. Democratic governments as well as dictatorial governments may be tyrannical; and a dictator, no less than a parliamentary assembly, may claim to voice the will of the people. The real question which should be asked is not whether the form of the government is democratic in the conventional sense, but whether the authority it exercises is absolute and arbitrary or whether it recognizes the existence of limits to that authority and is characterized by a fundamental respect for the rights of the individual; and in this sense democracy in Latin America is not meaningless. The Latin American countries have been subjected to arbitrary rule, but the demands which the rulers have made upon the ruled have rarely been total. Dictatorship has been formless rather than systematic. There is, indeed, a broad tolerance of life which has so far prohibited the organization in the New World of the totalitarian structures of the Old. The temperament of the Latin American peoples does not easily lend itself to regimentation, and in a very real sense democracy in Latin America has been, if not a form of government, at least a habit of mind and a climate of opinion.

Yet it remains true that the social structure of the majority of the Latin American states is profoundly undemocratic, and there can be no political democracy without a measure of social democracy. The patriarchal organization of colonial society has shown, indeed, an astonishing capacity for survival. The economy of all the Latin American countries is primarily an agrarian economy in which land-ownership means control of the major instrument of production.[1] The dominance of the *hacienda*, the great landed estate, has not only fostered the stratification of society; it has tended to perpetuate a concentration of political power in the hands of small minorities. Not only, moreover, in the Indian and mestizo countries, do the Indians themselves form a society within a society, and a society whose conduct is governed by a pattern of life and a scale of values fundamentally different from those of the surrounding civilizations, but throughout Latin America the educational and cultural level of the masses of the people and the general standards of public health are extraordinarily low. The average *per capita* income in Latin America is probably less than $100 a year, and in the cities as in the rural areas, except in a few favoured regions and industries, the standard of living of the urban and rural workers is often far below that required for the maintenance of a decent level of subsistence.[2]

These are not the conditions favourable to the growth of political democracy. The challenge to the traditional pattern of Latin American society, however, has been made, and the age-old struggle between town and country is being transformed into a clash between a new commercial

[1] Kingsley Davis, op. cit., p. 139.

[2] Cf. D. H. Blelloch, 'Labor Standards and Inter-American Solidarity', *Inter-American Quarterly*, iii (Oct. 1941), p. 58; and S. E. Harris, ed., *Economic Problems of Latin America* (New York and London, McGraw-Hill, 1944), pp. 4, 6, 27, 255.

and industrial civilization and an old agrarian way of life. The dominance of the *hacienda* has been directly challenged in Mexico; it is indirectly challenged elsewhere by the changing pattern of economic life and the rise of new social forces. It is true that the middle class in all the Latin American countries is still relatively small. It is true also that the number of Latin American workers who are effectively organized is by no means large, though the trade-union movement, under the guidance of the Confederation of Latin American Workers, now transcends state boundaries and is a force increasingly to be reckoned with. But the effect of these newer social forces is illustrated not merely by the enactment of labour codes, social insurance legislation, and national planning and development schemes,[1] but by the rise of new political parties; and it is significant that the twentieth-century Constitutions of Latin America all reflect, in more or less degree, a preoccupation with social problems as well as with political, and that labour legislation, partly no doubt for nationalistic reasons as well as social ones, preceded rather than followed trade union organization.

But the path of social reform, as experience has too tragically shown, may be the road to serfdom as well as freedom. It was a new and ominous element in Latin American life when some of the Latin American dictators, like the late President Busch of Bolivia, imported the language of National-Socialist doctrines; and the theory

[1] Cf. Blelloch, op .cit., together with his article on 'Latin America and the International Labour Standards', *International Labour Review*, xliii (1941), pp. 377–400; Ernesto Galarza, *Labor Trends and Social Welfare in Latin America, 1941 and 1942* (Washington, Pan American Union, 1943); R. A. Humphreys, 'Latin America and the Post-War World', *Agenda*, ii (1943), pp. 80–92; L. L. Lorwin, *National Planning in Selected Countries* (National Resources Planning Board, Technical Paper, No. 2, Washington, Government Printing Office, 1941).

that bad elections and good government are preferable to good elections and bad government is a dangerous one. Though, moreover, there has been evident an increasing approximation between constitutional aspirations and political practice, and a greater adaptation of political theory to social needs, the tendency in all the Latin American states is towards the concentration and centralization of power. The Constitutions reflect indeed the fear of presidential dictatorship; but the fact of presidential power is everywhere apparent, and even in the Federal Republics, though federalism is a theory, centralization is a fact. Finally, the problem of administrative efficiency, a problem which has long perplexed the Latin American countries in the absence, in most, of a highly trained, disinterested civil service, is more easily resolved, in the short run, by authority imposed from above rather than by that arising from below.

It is primarily to the operation of economic forces and to the rise of the new industrial aristocracy and the new middle class that such fusion as has been attained between the feudal and democratic traditions in the political fabric of Latin America has been due. On the capacity and honesty of these classes and of organized labour depends the extent to which that fusion can become complete. But it is foolish to assume that higher standards of living, bathrooms, refrigerators, and electric light, automatically make for democratic habits;[1] and meanwhile it would obviously be unwise to ignore the danger to the stability of existing insti-

---

[1] In *The Saturday Evening Post* (25 Dec. 1943) an official of the United States Government is quoted to the following effect: 'We can never be really friends with the Mexican people so long as most of them live as primitively as people did in the Middle Ages. Once they are able to live as we do, however; once they are able to eat meat regularly and keep their food in refrigerators and drink running water and read by electric lights, they will begin to think as we do, and friendship will automatically result.'

tutions or to the future of representative government arising from the 'extremist fringe' of politics,[1] on the Left and on the Right, and in that zone where Left and Right mingle, and exemplified in particular in so-called 'nationalist' groups, which draw their support from army leaders, old-fashioned Conservatives, current ideological doctrines, and idealistic or disillusioned youth.

It is in any event certain that nationalism, both political and economic, will be one of the forces moulding the future, and socialism another. But what direction these and other forces now at work in Latin American society will take it is impossible to foresee. Their manifestation is not uniform. It may be that the experience of Mexico will be repeated in some at least of the other republics and that suppressed social discontents will burst into conflagration. The forces of nationalism and socialism could be harnessed together in the service of the totalitarian state. It is possible also— and the experience of the past affords some hope for the future—that democratic development may follow the lines of traditional liberalism. The Latin American states are now a laboratory of political, social, and racial experiment, and the transformation which is in progress is only in its beginnings. Future developments depend not only on changing conditions in Latin America but on the conditions of world change. But the issue is no longer the simple issue of democracy or dictatorship; it is the larger issue of freedom or servitude.

[1] See J. C. Campbell, 'Political Extremes in South America', *Foreign Affairs*, xx (April 1942), pp. 517–34.

V

THE GREATER STATES OF LATIN AMERICA

I. ARGENTINA AND BRAZIL

ARGENTINA is the richest of the Latin American states. It has the highest *per capita* income.[1] It is, in proportion to its size and population, the most industrialized. It has long prided itself on being the most enlightened and progressive, and it earned in the present century, though perhaps too easily, a reputation as the most liberal and democratic. In *La Prensa* and *La Nación* it possesses newspapers the equal of any in the world, and in letters and in scholarship its intellectual life has displayed an increasing maturity.[2] It was, therefore, a shock when, in 1930, Argentina's constitutional evolution was violently disturbed, and a still more severe shock when, in 1943 and 1944, a series of palace and barrack-room revolutions reduced its political life to a mockery of democratic government.

Modern Argentina takes its rise from the eighteen-sixties, when the union of the Argentine provinces had at last been achieved under the Federal Constitution.[3] But, at the time of the first national census, in 1869, the whole population of the country was still under two millions. The plains Indians had not yet been subdued. The railways were in their infancy. On the pampa the ranges were unfenced.[4]

[1] Harris, *Economic Problems of Latin America*, p. 4, note 2.
[2] To some extent the maturity of a civilization may be judged by the sort of history it produces. The *Boletín del Instituto de Investigaciones Históricas*, the great *Historia de la Nación Argentina*, edited by the distinguished scholar, Ricardo Levene, and the impressive series of the *Documentos para la Historia Argentina*, published by the Faculty of Philosophy and Letters of the University of Buenos Aires, sufficiently illustrate the high quality of Argentine historical scholarship.   [3] *Ante*, p. 88.
[4] An Englishman, Richard Newton, put up the first wire fence in 1844, but it was only in the seventies that fencing was resorted to on a large and

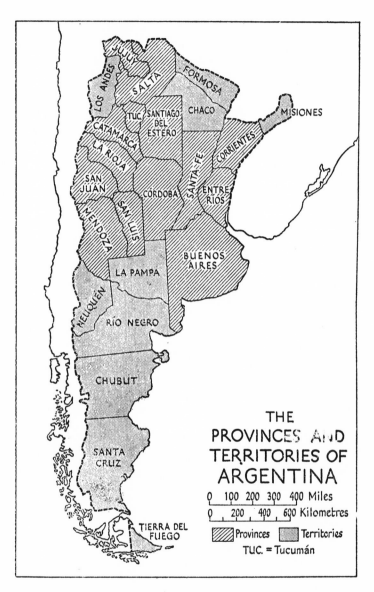

THE
PROVINCES AND
TERRITORIES OF
ARGENTINA

0 100 200 300 400 Miles
0 200 400 600 Kilometres

Provinces   Territories
TUC. = Tucumán

MAP 9

Sheep were more important than cattle. The area of tilled land was extraordinarily small. Cereals were still imported, not exported. 'Nowhere [else] in the world', Mark Jefferson has written, 'is there a land that has been colonized from Europe for three hundred years and still had to wait the arrival of newer Europeans to begin any effective use of its soil'.[1] The immigrant and immigrant capital, the railway network, barbed wire, the refrigerator ship and the *frigorí-fico*, these were the instruments of a pastoral, an agrarian, and a commercial revolution which converted the country into the world's greatest exporter of meat and one of its largest producers of grain, raised land values to fabulous heights, and transformed, with unprecedented rapidity, a backward frontier area into a highly urbanized commercial civilization.

A very few figures suffice to illustrate the rapidity of this change. Between 1869 and 1914 the population jumped from under two millions of people to nearly eight millions. The area of land under tillage increased from 0·13 acre *per capita* to 7·7 acres, a figure which compared with 1·5 acres in France and 4·8 acres in the United States.[2] The railways expanded from a bare 300 miles to a network of lines criss-crossing the pampa.[3] In 1880 pastoral products formed 90 per cent. of the country's exports; in 1903, for the first time, the value of the combined agricultural exports exceeded that of the combined pastoral exports.[4] Sheep-farming, meanwhile, became a frontier industry, extruded, by rising land values and the competition of

increasing scale. See S. G. Hanson, *Argentine Meat and the British Market* (Stanford Univ. Press, 1938), pp. 11–12.
[1] *Peopling the Argentine Pampa*, p. 45. [2] Ibid., pp. 43–4. *Ante*, p. 58.
[3] The development is graphically reproduced in R. García-Mata y Emilio Llorens, *Argentina Económica* (Buenos Aires, Cía Impresora Argentina, 1939), p. 132.
[4] Ibid., p. 156; Hanson, op. cit., pp. 120–1; James, *Latin America*, p. 345.

the cereal grower and the cattle man, to the drier margins of the pampa and to southern Patagonia, and the meat industry began its rapid rise. In 1876 the voyage of the *Frigorifique* had shown that meat could be transported across the tropics; six years later the first *frigorífico* was installed; there followed, in the nineties, a marked improvement in the breeding of herds to adapt Argentine meat to British taste; and with the expansion of the *frigoríficos* after 1900 the meat industry was fully launched. In 1905, for the first time, more beef arrived in England from Argentina than from the United States.[1]

The years from 1870 to 1914, however punctuated by crises, were the golden years of expansion. They were years of heavy immigration and rapid population growth, of expanding overseas markets and sources of supply of capital and manufactured goods. Yet already in the twenties immigration was declining, and in the thirties it almost ceased.[2] An economy had been developed, moreover, peculiarly dependent on widening channels of world trade. It received a shock, but only a temporary shock, during the war of 1914–18. But it was rudely and violently dislocated by the advent of the world depression in 1929. The prices of Argentine exports fell catastrophically, land values were halved, the cost of servicing the foreign debt was doubled.[3] These were the conditions under which Argentina's economy, more fortuitously than deliberately, underwent a new revolution, and this time an industrial revolution. The shortage of manufactured goods during the war of 1914–18 had indeed stimulated the growth of industriali-

---

[1] Hanson, op. cit., p. 141.   [2] *Ante*, p. 59.

[3] For the percentage fall of Latin American exports in terms of gold and United States dollars see W. Feuerlein and E. Hannan, *Dollars in Latin America* (New York, Council on Foreign Relations, 1941), p. 20. See also Ysabel Fisk and Robert A. Rennie, 'Argentina in Crisis', *Foreign Policy Reports*, xx (May 1944), p. 39.

zation, but it was in the nineteen-thirties that the movement attained to considerable proportions. Not only was
there a rapid increase in the number of persons engaged in
industrial pursuits, but between 1935 and 1942 the value
of industrial production doubled, and, whereas, in 1903,
the value of agricultural exports had equalled the value of
pastoral exports, in 1942 the net value of industrial production equalled that of agricultural and pastoral production.[1]

This was a new and remarkable change in the pattern of
Argentina's economic life. Its significance is enhanced
by reason of the fact that the proportion of the rural to
the urban population of Argentina has been steadily declining, so that already by 1938 the urban population
represented nearly three-quarters of the whole.[2] Yet
Argentina possesses neither coal nor iron in any significant
quantities, and, so far as is known, no great or easily
available reserves of oil[3] or hydro-electric power. Despite
the riches with which nature has endowed her, she has few
of the industrial potentialities of Brazil, and her Middle
West lacks the complement of the United States industrial
east. Nor, in reverse, is there a large rural market, under
present conditions of agriculture and stock-raising, for the
continued expansion of Argentine light industries. This is
the explanation of Argentine interest in the resources of

[1] Harris, op. cit., p. 227; Banco Central de la República Argentina,
Annual Report (Buenos Aires, 1943), pp. 4–6. For the development of Argentine industry see Adolfo Dorfman, *Evolución Industrial Argentina* (Buenos
Aires, Editorial Losada, 1942). According to the *Estadística Industrial de
1941*, published by the Dirección General de Estadística y Censos de la
Nación (Buenos Aires, 1944), p. 19, 829,700 persons were employed in
industry in 1941 as against 538,489 in 1935.

[2] R. García-Mata y E. Llorens, op. cit., p. 14.

[3] Despite the oilfields of Comodoro Rivadavia and Plaza Huincul, both
in Patagonia, and the fields in Mendoza and Salta. New sources, however,
may be discovered.

Chile, Bolivia, and Paraguay, of her designs for a customs union with Chile and Paraguay, and of her continued economic penetration of Bolivia. Despite her material prosperity, Argentina has arrived at a crisis in her national development. The future is no longer the unclouded future of the early years of the century, but an uncertain future dependent not only on the conditions of the outside world but on a readjustment between the fundamental elements in the nation's internal economy—agriculture, stock-raising, industry—and on the extent to which Argentina can achieve a higher standard of living for her rural and urban masses.

In this changing pattern of economic life, with its inevitable repercussions on the traditional structure of society, lies in part the explanation of the political vicissitudes of the country's recent past. The last of Argentina's problems of national organization was settled in 1880. The Federal Constitution had been adopted in 1853. Buenos Aires accepted it, to dominate it, in 1861. In 1880 the too powerful province, after a brief civil war, was shorn of its capital city, and the city itself became the federal district under the direct control of the Federal Government. Thenceforth Argentine political life took a new direction. The political struggle no longer turned on the old quarrel between the one and the thirteen that had dominated the early history of the republic. It was now concerned with the adaptation of the Constitution to the needs of a rapidly changing society. The oligarchy that ruled in 1880 had produced a series of able and distinguished presidents—Bartolomé Mitre, Sarmiento, Avellaneda, Roca, all men of high abilities. But two tendencies were clearly apparent. The first was for the Federal Government, and within the Federal Government the President, to dominate the life of the Federation. The second was for the small landed aristocracy, the governing oligarchy, to perpetuate its own monopoly of power.

During the next fifty years these tendencies were accentuated rather than diminished. Even in the United States, where an attachment to states-rights is genuine and profound, the most pronounced feature of constitutional change since the Civil War has been the extension of the powers of the national Government at the expense of the several states. In Argentina this process was carried to far greater lengths. The provinces, or most of them, became, and have remained, 'obscure satellites' of the Federal Government.[1] Greater Buenos Aires contains more than a quarter of the whole population of Argentina; and within a comparatively small area, of which Buenos Aires is the hub, is concentrated the bulk of the country's agricultural, pastoral, and industrial wealth.[2] Inevitably, the well-to-do and the socially and politically ambitious were drawn to the federal capital, and provincial life was denuded of its talent. Inevitably, the provinces looked to the Federal Treasury for financial assistance on federal terms. The Constitution, moreover, itself endowed the Federal Government with a direct means of nullifying their autonomy. The right granted to the federal authorities to intervene in provincial affairs to guarantee the republican form of government, or to support or re-establish the constituted authorities on

[1] A. F. Macdonald, *Government of the Argentine Republic* (New York, Crowell, 1942), p. 156.

[2] This is the zone of the 'litoral' or the humid pampa. It includes the Province of Buenos Aires, a part of the Pampa territory, the east and south of Córdoba, the centre and south of Santa Fe, Entre Ríos, and a small part of Corrientes. It comprises about 22 per cent. of the total area of the country, but accounts for 68 per cent. of the population, 70 per cent. of the railway lines, 84 per cent. of the motor-cars, 86 per cent. of the cereal and flax area, 62 per cent. of the cattle, and 85 per cent. of the industrial production. E. Llorens and R. García-Mata, 'Regiones Naturales de La Argentina', *Revista de Economía Argentina,* xxxix (May 1940), pp. 145–51.

their request, has been used with none of the restraint with which a similar but narrower power has been employed by the Federal Government in the United States. Between 1860 and 1940 the weapon of intervention was resorted to 129 times. General Uriburu, who seized power in 1930, intervened in twelve provinces within a week,[1] and the military rulers who, after the *coup d'état* of June 1943, hastened to replace the governors of the provinces by military interventors merely acted according to well-worn precedent. It was only the apparently inexhaustible supply of colonels to fill these and other posts that was new.

The autonomy of most of the provinces has thus been reduced to little more than a fiction, and the party in control of the Federal Government has been enabled to manipulate provincial politics much according to its will. But there is a further feature of this extension of federal powers. In the scheme of Argentine political life the President was cast for a part still more important than that played by the President of the United States.[2] Every extension of federal authority has enhanced the vast powers inherent in the Presidency. The President both reigns and governs. The majority of provincial interventions have taken place under simple executive decree, and it is only a further illustration of this presidential prepotency that from December 1941 till his overthrow in June 1943 Acting-President, and later President, Castillo governed under the conditions of a state of siege, by the proclamation of which constitutional guarantees are virtually suspended, though not necessarily unregarded.

It is difficult to decide whether the political abuse of legitimate powers is the cause or the effect of the indifference with which the majority of Argentines have been apt to

[1] Macdonald, op. cit., pp. 170–1.   [2] Ibid., p. 190.

regard the conduct of public affairs. Certainly these abuses have not been confined to any one political party. Nevertheless one party, or rather one group of vested interests, has enjoyed, with a brief interval of fourteen years, a dominance of power. In the nineteenth century it has been estimated that 400 peers owned between one-fifth and one-sixth of the total acreage of the United Kingdom.[1] This was an excessive concentration of landownership in the hands of a few families. In Argentina, however, in 1940, 221 persons, together with 51 land companies, still owned one-sixth of the Province of Buenos Aires, the richest of all the Argentine provinces.[2] The great estates are now in process of decay. But in 1944, 62 per cent. of all the farms in the country were still worked by tenants or share croppers.[3] It is customary in Argentina to speak of the 2,000 land-owning families. It was this small oligarchy which ruled Argentina in 1880 and, under the name of the National Autonomist Party, continued to rule till 1916. Under the régime which it perfected the President nominated his successor, the provincial governors, the members of Congress, and almost everyone else. Elections were the merest of formalities, and the path of opposition was the path of revolution.

This system was first challenged in 1890, when the Civic Union was organized as a protest against governmental corruption. This, in turn, led to the creation of the Radical Civic Union, the ancestor of the Radical party, in 1892. The organization of the Socialist party followed in 1896.

---

[1] A. S. Turberville, 'The House of Lords and the Advent of Democracy, 1837-67', *History* (New Series), xxix (1944), p. 164.

[2] *Revista de Economía Argentina*, xli (Sept. 1942), p. 290. For conditions in other of the Argentine provinces see George Soule, David Efron, and Norman T. Ness, *Latin America in the Future World* (New York, Farrar and Rinehart, 1945), pp. 71-2.

[3] *Revista de Economía Argentina*, xliii (Sept. 1944), p. 286.

For the next twenty years the Radical Civic Union devoted itself to the seemingly hopeless cause of electoral reform, a cause suddenly and astonishingly realized when, in 1912, President Roque Sáenz Peña personally insisted on the enactment of the famous law, which bears his name, of the secret and obligatory vote. The result, in the first free presidential elections in Argentine history, in 1916, was the triumph of the Radicals, and the elevation of their leader, Hipólito Irigoyen, to the Presidency.

Argentina remained under Radical rule till 1930. The term is, of course, a misnomer. The Radicals were, and are, no more radical than nineteenth-century Whigs. They took office as a middle-class, progressive party of reform; but office is a corrupting influence, and certainly in their latter days the energies of the Radicals were devoted to consolidating their power by methods as dubious as any of those employed by the Conservatives. Electoral freedom, under Radical rule, was permitted, but it was freedom within a narrow range. Irigoyen himself outdid most of his predecessors in the number of his provincial interventions, and it is an illustration of the weakness of Argentine political parties and of their lack of a coherent structure that, more and more, he governed as a personal ruler. When, in 1922, he nominated his successor, it was inevitable that the party should split into two wings, a 'personalist' and an 'anti-personalist' wing. Yet the period from 1912 to 1928 saw a progressive liberalization of Argentine politics. The tragedy was that when in 1928 Irigoyen was re-elected to the Presidency, by an unprecedented majority, he was an aged dreamer. The President shrouded himself in mystery. He was surrounded by obscure politicians. Graft returned to government offices; administrative efficiency was gravely impaired; and at the moment when the world economic crisis overtook Argentina, her government was threatened with paralysis at the extremities and apoplexy at the centre.[1]

The revolution of September 1930 ended this situation. It was bloodless and astonishingly popular,[2] but it enabled the Conservatives with the aid of the military to re-establish their power. A state of siege was declared. Radical leaders were imprisoned or exiled. Elections were staged in November 1931, when General Justo became President. Six years later General Justo nominated his successor, Dr. Ortiz, and when Dr. Ortiz professed his intention of leading the country back on the road to electoral liberty, ill health intervened. In July 1940 the President was compelled to delegate his powers to the Vice-President, Dr. Castillo. A stern, unbending Tory, Dr. Castillo was determined at all costs to prevent the return of the Radicals. They had already, under the more austere government of Dr. Ortiz, obtained control of the House of Representatives, and although not the Radicals but the Socialists were the strongest party in Buenos Aires itself, there was no doubt that the Radicals enjoyed the largest popular following in the country at large. But from Dr. Castillo they had nothing to hope. The one point on which the Government coalition of National Democrats and Anti-Personalist Radicals was resolute was to maintain all power in its own hands. To that end, foreign and domestic policy were alike subordinated, and it was only the *coup d'état* of June 1943 which prevented Dr. Castillo from imposing his successor on the country.

The *coup d'état* of 1943, and the governments that fol-

---

[1] See A. Hasbrouck, 'The Argentine Revolution of 1930', *Hispanic American Historical Review*, xviii (1938), pp. 285–321. See also Ernest Galarza, 'Argentina's Revolution and its Aftermath', *Foreign Policy Reports*, vii (Oct. 1931), pp. 309–22.   [2] Hasbrouck, op. cit., p. 319.

lowed it, were the price that Argentines paid for the counter-revolution of 1930, for the fraudulence and corruption of public life, for the lack of honesty among the political parties (the Socialists are a notable exception), for a too easily won material prosperity,[1] and for failure to adapt the structure of politics to the structure of society. If faith is dead and honour dies, the door is opened to new and alien political creeds, to government by the 'extremist fringe', or by military adventurers and ambitious demagogues. The humiliation to the Argentine people was profound. But it is well to recall Lord Bryce's description of the greatest democracy of modern times in the eighteen-eighties, and the ingenuous delegate who, at one of the National Conventions at Chicago, inquired 'What are we here for except the offices?'[2] There is no occasion to despair of democracy in Argentina, and these events may yet prove to have been one of those shocks which make a turning-point in the life of a nation.

There was, however, a further element which contributed to this domestic crisis. That element was the additional confusion imported into Argentine public life by the neutrality policy studiously pursued by the Castillo Government, and the sudden awakening on the part of so-called 'Nationalists' to a changing balance of forces on the South American continent. During the nineteenth century Argentina and Brazil had continued in Latin America the former colonial rivalries of Spain and Portugal. The interests of both Powers clashed as well as coincided in the area of the River Plate, and each for long felt free to intervene in the buffer state of Uruguay to attain its own

[1] See a remarkable leading article in *La Prensa*, 28 Sept. 1944. For the *coup d'état* see *Inter-American Affairs, 1943*, ed. A. P. Whitaker (New York, Columbia Univ. Press, 1944), pp. 23 ff., and Ray Josephs, *Argentine Diary* (New York, Random House, 1944).

[2] *The American Commonwealth* (3 vols., London, 1888), ii. 455.

particular ends.[1] For most of the century, however, the Brazilian Empire enjoyed in South America a position of unquestioned primacy, and it was not till the fall of the empire in 1889 that this position was challenged by Argentina. Thenceforth Argentina began to claim for herself the political leadership of Latin America, not only, indeed, as against Brazil but as against the United States. The war of 1914–18 momentarily restored the older balance. As the greatest of the Latin American states involved in the war, Brazil, at Versailles, resumed her old political position, and it was notable that Argentina withdrew from the League of Nations in 1920 and did not resume participation till after Brazil had herself withdrawn in 1926.[2] But this restoration was only temporary. It was not till the late nineteen-thirties and, more particularly, till the political, strategic, and economic consequences of the second World War were fully felt, that the balance of power again began to shift in favour of Brazil. Brazil, in 1942, for a second time entered a world conflict. Her resources were mobilized on behalf of the United Nations. Her production was expanded. Lend-Lease equipment was made available; air and naval bases were improved. Economic and military potential alike increased. Argentina, on the other hand, still maintained diplomatic relations with the Axis. Resolute in her neutrality, she rested in self-imposed isolation; and there can be little doubt that Argentines watched, with growing concern, the relative decline in Argentina's power in comparison with that of Brazil, and that this concern played its part in the *coup d'état* of June 1943.[3]

Brazil contains nearly half the population of the southern continent. Most of this is concentrated in what is barely

---

[1] The best short account of these international rivalries in the River Plate is in Haring, *South American Progress*, pp. 91–105.   [2] She did not resume full participation till 1933.   [3] Whitaker, op. cit., p. 23.

more than a seaboard strip to the north and east, and in a deeper southern zone. Two-thirds of the entire area, Brazil's Middle and Far West, is almost devoid of people.[1] A fringe of civilization, but only a fringe, borders the great 'bulge of Brazil', where sugar was first king and then cotton.[2] But it is the southern region, from Minas Gerais and Espírito Santo to Rio Grande do Sul, which dominates Brazil much as the humid pampa dominates Argentina. With one-sixth of the land area it has more than half the population. It is here that the majority of Brazilian immigrants have settled, and it is this region which accounts for the bulk of Brazilian agricultural and industrial production.[3]

The resources of Brazil, however, are so vast that they have yet been scarcely touched. Her westward movement is still only in its beginnings; and not only are great tracts of land suitable for agriculture and stock-raising yet unsettled,[4] but Brazil possesses what Argentina lacks, great reserves of mineral wealth. She is, it is true, deficient in supplies of high-grade coal. Her known supplies of oil are even less extensive than those of Argentina. But, together with an abundance of other metals, she has the largest reserves of iron-ore in the world and great potential resources of hydro-electric power. Not want of land or want of natural wealth has retarded Brazilian economic development, but want of labour and want of capital, and

[1] The states of Pará, Amazonas, Mato Grosso, and Goiaz, the territories of Amapá, Rio Branco, Acre, Guaporé, and Ponta Porã, and parts of Maranhão, Piauí, and Baía.

[2] See Normano, *Brazil, a Study of Economic Types*, pp. 18–35.

[3] In 1938 it accounted for 85 per cent. of the agricultural output and 88 per cent. of the industrial, and contained 74 per cent. of the railways, 67 per cent. of the roads, 87 per cent. of the vehicles, 90 per cent. of the electric power, and 89 per cent. of the factories. See M. L. Cooke, *Brazil on the March—a Study in International Co-operation* (New York and London, McGraw-Hill, 1944), p. 36; Harris, op. cit., p. 276. There are some useful statistics in *Brazil, 1939–40, an Economic, Social and Geographical Survey* (Rio de Janeiro, Ministry of Foreign Affairs, 1940).   [4] *Ante*, pp. 7–8, 75.

the fact that for four hundred years the economy of the country was dominated by a series of mono-cultures, sugar, cacao, gold, tobacco, cotton, rubber, coffee. 'Its leitmotif', as J. A. Normano has written, was 'the perpetual change of the "kings"', a perpetual alternation of leading

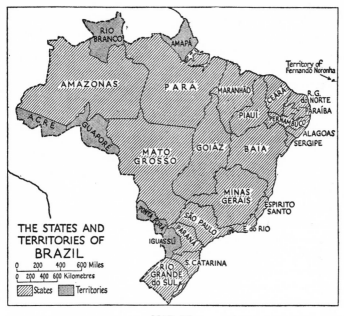

THE STATES AND
TERRITORIES OF
BRAZIL

0   200   400   600 Miles
0 200 400 600 Kilometres
▨ States   ▦ Territories

MAP 10

products, accompanied by a perpetual recurrence of booms and slumps. The fruit was too easily plucked; wealth too easily won.

In the nineteenth century a plantation system based on slave labour as effectually prevented the diversification of the Brazilian economy as it did that of the southern states of the United States. Only with the abolition of slavery in 1888, and under the stimulus of heavy immigration, could any significant change in the pattern of economic development occur. A wage system replaced a slave system. The *fazendeiro*, the great planter, was the mainstay of the empire; but empire and republic were contrasting ways of economic life as well as contrasting forms of political organization. 'The sugar and plantation economy was the background of the leadership of Bahia and Pernambuco in the empire; coffee and industrial progress, that of São Paulo during the first Republic';[1] and it was with the republic that the modern evolution of Brazil began.

The change was comparable to the contemporary development in Argentina. Between 1890 and 1914 the population almost doubled; the railways expanded from under 6,000 to nearly 15,000 miles of track; industry, almost non-existent in 1890, gained its first precarious foothold.[2] This was the beginning of an economic revolution still in progress. The war of 1914–18, by severely curtailing Brazilian imports, much accelerated it. In 1914 Brazil still imported almost all the industrial products she consumed. But within the next four years the value of the nation's industrial production more than doubled;[3] and between the two wars the industrial evolution of the country, thus begun, rapidly continued. Already by 1938 the value of industrial production had outstripped the value of agricultural production,[4] and between 1938 and 1942 the number of 'industrial establishments'[5] rose from 60,000 to more than 80,000 and the number of industrial

[1] Normano, op. cit., p. 55.
[2] Some 7,000 industrial 'establishments' originated between 1890 and 1914. Ibid., p. 99.   [3] Ibid., pp. 103–5; Harris, op. cit., p. 277.
[4] Cooke, op. cit., p. 40; Harris, op. cit., p. 278.
[5] *Fortnightly Review*, Bank of London and South America, 10 June 1944. The textile and food-processing industries are the most important. See also José Jobim, *Brazil in the Making* (New York, Macmillan, 1943), pp. 93–9.

workers to more than a million. When, moreover, in 1941-2, work was begun on the great Volta Redonda steel plant in the State of Rio de Janeiro, that fact was interpreted in Brazil not only as perhaps the most important single event in the economic history of the country, but as something in the nature of a declaration of economic independence. Brazil is still primarily an agricultural country. In 1938 two-thirds of the employed population were engaged in agriculture and stock-raising.[1] But it is an agriculture increasingly diversified and an economy in which industry is destined to play an increasing part. The changed economic status of Brazil is a fact; and despite grave deficiencies of labour and transport, of sources of power and sources of capital, and despite also the low standard of living of the masses of the people, it is possible, as Mr. Henry Wallace once prophesied of Latin America as a whole, that Brazil is about to enter upon a period of economic development comparable to that experienced by the United States during the last fifty years.

It is astonishing that so huge and thinly peopled a state as Brazil should have so well preserved its unity and even, by peaceful means, have added to its territorial extent. Had the early system of hereditary captaincies, based on natural geographic divisions, survived, it is possible, even probable, that Portuguese America, like Spanish America, would have disintegrated into a number of independent units.[2] Had the Crown, in 1808, not itself transferred the seat of government from Lisbon to Rio de Janeiro, it is still possible that Brazil would not have preserved its unity. The fact that it was so preserved is a service that Brazil owes to the

[1] R. Paula Lopes, 'Social Problems and Legislation in Brazil', *International Labour Review*, xliv (1941), p. 497.

[2] P. A. Martin, 'Federalism in Brazil', *Hispanic American Historical Review*, xviii (1938), p. 144; J. P. Calogeras, *A History of Brazil* (trans. and ed. by P. A. Martin, Chapel Hill, Univ. of North Carolina Press, 1939), p. 10.

empire. It was as a centralized unitary monarchy that Brazil began its independent life. The provinces, under the Constitution of 1824, were little more than administrative units. They were given, in 1834, a somewhat greater degree of autonomy, after, in 1831, the first Emperor, Dom Pedro I, too absolutist in tone, too dissolute in manners, and too much under the influence of the old Portuguese element, for the liking of the Brazilian aristocracy, had been forced from the throne. But this autonomy was again abridged in view of widespread signs of separatism and actual disorder; and when in 1847 the Emperor Pedro II began to govern as well as reign (he was only twenty-two), the system he inherited had been little changed.[1]

Dom Pedro 'reigned, governed and administered' till 1889.[2] Under him the empire developed peaceful quasi-parliamentary institutions. The forms of constitutionalism were strictly observed. The Emperor's own high-mindedness was never questioned. His influence was wholly benevolent and his rule the most liberal that Brazil has seen. Yet in 1889 the empire suddenly collapsed. It is true that the abolition of slavery without compensation to the slave-owners had offended the great landlords. It is true that the Church had become increasingly alienated by the Emperor's liberal principles. It is true that the old desire of the provinces for greater autonomy had grown increasingly strong. But it was a combination of academic republicanism and military discontent which precipitated a sudden and spectacular fall,[3] which surprised Brazilians, perhaps, as much as the rest of the world.

[1] A. K. Manchester, 'Constitutional Dictatorship in Brazil', in Wilgus, op. cit., p. 443.
[2] The best biography is M. W. Williams, *Dom Pedro the Magnanimous, Second Emperor of Brazil* (Chapel Hill, Univ. of North Carolina Press, 1937).
[3] See P. A. Martin, 'Causes of the Collapse of the Brazilian Empire', *Hispanic American Historical Review*, iv (1921), pp. 4–48.

The centralized unitary monarchy was now replaced by the federal republic and a parliamentary by a presidential system. The Constitution of 1891, which was to survive for nearly forty years, was frankly modelled on that of the United States. But though the old provinces, now states, were endowed with a far greater degree of autonomy than the several states of the United States,[1] in fact it was still the central government and still the central executive which exercised the preponderant power. It has become the fashion, since the Liberal Republic was overthrown in 1930, to regard it as a travesty of constitutional government under which the country was racked by intolerable inter-state rivalries, provincial politics, and competing economic interests. This is exaggeration. It is, however, true that an oligarchy ruled, as an oligarchy always has ruled Brazil, but an oligarchy now wider than that of the landowning aristocracy of the empire, and an oligarchy distinguished by the ability of its political leaders. It is also true that two states, São Paulo and Minas Gerais, enjoyed a monopoly of political power, and, by an amicable arrangement, shared the Presidency, alternately, between them. Nor is it to be supposed that elections conformed to the highest standards of purity.

Brazilians, however, are attached to the forms of constitutionalism, and in 1930 the forms of constitutionalism vanished. The revolution of that year, which swept Dr. Getulio Vargas, of Rio Grande do Sul, into power, was a protest against São Paulo's continued domination of national politics. Thereafter, not São Paulo, but Dr. Vargas, ruled Brazil, if not unchallenged, at least undisturbed. The Constitution of 1891 was suspended. Federal, state, and municipal assemblies were dissolved. State

[1] See H. G. James, *The Constitutional System of Brazil* (Washington, Carnegie Institution, 1923).

governors were replaced by federal interventors. Executive and legislative functions were united in the President, who was empowered to govern by decree until a duly elected Constituent Assembly should deliberate on the constitutional reorganization of the country.[1] São Paulo, unwilling to surrender its traditional pre-eminence, rose in revolt in 1932, and was only defeated after more than two months of civil war; but Dr. Vargas was careful to treat the rebellious state with studious moderation; and he proceeded in 1933 to summon a Constituent Assembly which promulgated in July 1934 the second Constitution of the Brazilian Republic.

The Constitution of 1934 was a link between the Liberal Constitution of 1891 and the frankly authoritarian Constitution of 1937; and the Constituent Assembly amiably designated Dr. Vargas as the first President under the new régime, though the powers of the President were defined and presidential re-election was forbidden. In 1935, however, after revolts in the states of Rio Grande do Norte, Rio de Janeiro, and Pernambuco (alleged to be Communist-inspired) Congress passed a constitutional amendment under which the President might, when necessary, be authorized to declare 'a state of grave internal commotion', during which constitutional guarantees would be suspended.[2] In 1937, as the end of Dr. Vargas's term came in sight and preparations for presidential elections were in hand, Congress authorized the President to use this power on grounds of an alleged danger of an imminent Communist rising. On 10 November troops surrounded the seat of Congress; Congress was dissolved; and a new Constitution was miraculously produced. Shortly afterwards, the governors of almost all the states were replaced by federal interventors, and in December all political parties were dissolved.

[1] K. Loewenstein, *Brazil under Vargas* (New York, Macmillan, 1942), p. 18.　　　　[2] Ibid., pp. 28–9.

From then till 1945 Dr. Vargas ruled in complete if benevolent despotism. An attempted uprising in May 1938 by the Integralists, the native Fascist party, whom the President had at one time appeared to favour, was the last serious threat to his régime. Meanwhile the authoritarian Constitution of 1937, of which Sr. Francisco Campos' was the ingenious author, failed to be put into operation. One article of the transitory provisions of the Constitution declared a state of emergency to exist, and during such a state those parts of the Constitution as the President might choose were suspended. By a further article all legislative bodies, federal, state, and municipal, were dissolved, and elections for a new Parliament were not to take place till the Constitution was ratified by a plebiscite. No plebiscite, however, was held; the state of emergency was maintained; and Dr. Vargas continued to govern by decree. It was only on 28 February 1945 that a constitutional amendment was promulgated, providing for the direct election of the President, the Chamber of Deputies, the Federal Council, and the state governors, and stating that the time had arrived when it was essential to put into operation the representative institutions which even the Constitution of 1937 envisaged.

Dr. Vargas was supported by no party organization; he made no attempt to create such an organization. There was no specific creed attached to his régime. It was a civil, not a military régime; and the tolerance of Brazilians, so marked a feature of the empire as of the republic, itself set bounds to the dictatorship. National in origin and nationalist in purpose, it indulged in little of the regimentation of the totalitarian state. Dom Pedro used to avow that he would be a republican if he were not a monarch; Dr. Vargas might well have said that he would be a democrat were he not a dictator; and certainly, like Dom Pedro, Dr. Vargas has played no small part in the creation of the Brazilian nation.

MAP II

VI

THE GREATER STATES OF LATIN AMERICA

II. CHILE AND MEXICO

O N the west coast of South America control of the sea has meant control of the land. Control of the sea enabled Chile in the war of the Pacific (1879–83) to defeat the combined forces of Peru and Bolivia and to deprive the former of her rich nitrate province of Tarapacá and the latter of her Pacific coastline. Control of the sea enabled the Chilean Congress to defeat the Chilean President in the most famous civil war in Chilean history in 1891; and control of the sea, together with the possession of the rich mineral resources of her newly won desert north, assured for Chile in the half-century after the war of the Pacific a position of pre-eminence on the west coast of South America comparable to that of Argentina on the east.

There were, however, other reasons for this pre-eminence. Chile, in the nineteenth century, was, after Brazil, politically the most stable, as well as economically one of the most prosperous, of Latin American states. The civil war of 1891 was the one great, and the only disastrous, interlude in the ordered, or relatively ordered, sequence of her constitutional life between the adoption of the Constitution of 1833 and its overthrow in 1924. Wealth, government, education, were the preserve of a small, omnipotent, landed oligarchy. In return, the oligarchy gave to Chile internal peace and the outward forms if not the inner meaning of parliamentary government.

The early years of the republic had been turbulent enough. Emancipated, reconquered, again liberated, the country was torn between competing theories of government and rival aspirants to govern. It moved from an extreme of centralization, under the Supreme Directorship of Bernardo O'Higgins, the illegitimate son of a poor Irish boy who had risen in the service of Spain to the high eminence of Viceroy of Peru, to an extreme of decentralization. It was racked by factional strife. But geography imposed a natural unity on Chile. Between the Andes and the sea, and between an arid north and a rain-drenched south, central Chile is a region somewhat smaller than England and Scotland, blessed by a Mediterranean climate and by a fertile central valley. This was the heart of colonial Chile, and it is still the core of the modern republic. It contained perhaps half a million people in 1800 and perhaps a million in 1830.[1] The social organization of this isolated, relatively small, relatively compact community was, moreover, extraordinarily rigid. It was a society in which a landed aristocracy ruled and a landless peasantry obeyed, in which the peasant was bound to the soil by contract or custom, and in which the great landed estate was the fundamental territorial, economic, and social unit.[2]

For this society independence meant divorce from Spain but not from Spanish institutions.[3] The revolution was a political, not a social, revolution. That 'adorable equality', which the youthful O'Higgins had once confessed to be his idol,[4] was far from the taste of the creole aristocracy, which lived in patriarchal splendour on their rural domains, asked only to order the country at large as they ordered their estates, and were certainly not disposed to tolerate any far-

---

[1] Miguel Cruchaga, *Estudio sobre la Organización Económica i la Hacienda Pública de Chile* (2 vols., Santiago, 1878–81), i. 147, 151, 274.

[2] McBride, *Chile: Land and Society*, pp. 120–1.

[3] Ibid., p. 188; Luis Galdames, *A History of Chile* (trans. and ed. by I. J. Cox, Chapel Hill, Univ. of North Carolina Press, 1941), p. 204.

[4] Ernesto de la Cruz, *Epistolario de D. Bernardo O'Higgins* (2 vols., Madrid, Biblioteca Ayacucho, 1920), i. 39.

reaching innovations in the structure of property, religion, and law. It was this conservative oligarchy which contrived, in 1823, the fall of O'Higgins. It submitted, in 1830, to the dictatorship of Diego Portales,[1] as a means of securing the organization of the republic on solid and lasting foundations, and, in the Constitution of 1833, it devised an instrument which perpetuated its power for close on a century.

The Constitution of 1833 was, indeed, coldly realistic. The illiterate and the property-less—that is, the greater part of the population—were excluded from the franchise. Provincial and local administration were made directly to depend on the central government, and, within the central government, so great were the powers placed in the hands of the President that the system which prevailed during the first thirty years of the operation of the Constitution was little short of an autocracy. The President, in the words of Luis Galdames,

'not only directed the administration of the country, but controlled the congressional elections and appointed his successor. The courts of justice, the army and the navy as well, and all public functionaries depended directly on him; and the intendants and governors—his immediate representatives in the provinces—with the police and alcaldes of their jurisdiction, held the entire nation in one single net of authority.'[2]

So long as Chile was, in effect, a one-party state and the President represented the interests of the oligarchy, this system worked fairly well. It was, on the whole, a system of order, characterized by severity, but characterized also by a moderate respect for the outward forms of constitutionalism; and, by it, Chile was saved from the *caudillismo*

[1] See L. W. Bealer, 'Diego Portales, Dictator and Organizer of Chile', in Wilgus, *South American Dictators*, pp. 173–86.
[2] Galdames, op. cit., p. 361.

of her neighbours. But no Dame Partington and her mop, in the shape of Don Diego Portales and the Constitution of 1833, could indefinitely arrest the tide of change, and by the middle of the century the oligarchy had ceased to be united. Government was still government of the masses by the classes.[1] But a new Liberal party challenged Conservative rule. The Radicals (alarming more in name than policy) in turn gradually divided from the Liberals, while the vexed problems of the relations of Church and State began to transform the Conservatives into a clerical, ultramontane party.[2] Congress, moreover, or the divisions among the ruling caste within it, now attempted to assert control over the executive, and behind the façade of the presidential system there grew up what President Balmaceda described as a 'new idea' of parliamentary government, 'a mere pretext', he asserted, 'of discontented factions to work out their own ends'.[3]

This sweeping condemnation of parliamentarianism in Chile was, no doubt, a partial view; but the issue thus raised between the executive and the legislature was fundamental. It came suddenly and decisively to a head in 1890–1. President Balmaceda,[4] a Radical Tory, stood for a strict interpretation of the Constitution, together with a programme of reform by no means acceptable to Congress; and, but for one final unconstitutional act, his interpretation of his prerogatives was supported by the letter of the law. Congress, on the other hand, upholding the theory of ministerial responsibility and those privileges of parliamentary control which it had increasingly arrogated to itself, was sustained by custom and convention. The con-

---

[1] M. H. Hervey, *Dark Days in Chile* (London, 1891–2), p. 305.
[2] Galdames, op. cit., p. 317.   [3] Hervey, op. cit., p. 91.
[4] See L. W. Bealer, 'Balmaceda, Liberal Dictator of Chile', in Wilgus, op. cit., pp. 198–211.

flict, which ended in civil war and the suicide of the President, was only superficially a conflict between dictatorial and popular government. In such terms it is difficult to decide which of the protagonists was the less popular or, strictly speaking, the more unconstitutional. But the result was clear and definite. The omnipotence of the legislature replaced the omnipotence of the executive. Henceforth Congress controlled the Cabinet while the executive lacked that safeguard of parliamentary government—the right to dissolve the legislature. Presidential intervention in elections ceased, but elections did not thereby become free; and the political parties which, in the United States, alone enabled the presidential and federal system to function efficiently, in Chile first destroyed the presidential system and then failed to operate a parliamentary one. So rapidly did their number increase that none had power to govern by itself. Governments were coalition governments. Cabinets were made and fell, parties combined and divided with bewildering and fatal facility; and however interesting this pseudo-parliamentary régime as an experiment in pure politics,[1] it was not responsible nor democratic nor even efficient government that it provided.

Not merely, however, was the Government, during the thirty years after the civil war of 1891, characterized by the extreme instability of ministries and a high degree of irresponsibility; the structure of politics ceased to correspond with the structure of society. The dominance of the *hacienda* remained complete. The bulk of the population was still landless or restricted to unprofitable holdings. A few families monopolized the agricultural land,[2] and so

[1] See P. S. Reinsch, 'Parliamentary Government in Chile', *American Political Science Review*, iii (1908–9), pp. 507–38.

[2] McBride, op. cit., pp. 124–32, 144; C. A. Thomson, 'Chile Struggles for National Recovery', *Foreign Policy Reports*, ix (Feb. 1934), pp. 286–7. *Ante*, p. 56.

inefficient was the agrarian system that Chile, essentially an agricultural country, was compelled to import agricultural produce. The desert north, which contained the world's only considerable deposits of natural nitrates, not the agricultural Central Valley, was the source of the country's wealth. Nitrates and copper, industries controlled from abroad, dominated the export trade and provided the greater part of the government revenues; and industrial development in the nitrate fields, in the copper and coal mines, and to some degree also in the cities, fostered the growth of a new middle class and a new industrial proletariat. In south-central Chile a new and independent class of smallholders had made their appearance, pioneers of the frontier.[1] In the northern provinces society, agricultural and industrial, was free from the shackles of the *hacienda*. In central Chile the landowners ceased to be the patriarchal rulers of their estates and surrendered their strength by becoming absentee rentiers; and in the towns the new industrial proletariat knew nothing of the old feudal relationship of *patrón* and client, landowner and labourer.[2]

The challenge thus presented to the traditional order of society was strengthened by the rapid growth of popular education on the one hand (a development much to the credit of the oligarchy) and by social distress on the other. The new middle class and the new industrial proletariat, living at little more than subsistence levels, were victimized by persistent currency depreciation and a rising cost of living. They were peculiarly dependent on the varying fortunes of the country's two leading exports, copper and

[1] *Ante*, p. 68.
[2] Thomson, op. cit., pp. 282–3; McBride, op. cit., p. 369; C. H. Haring, 'Chilean Politics, 1920–1928', *Hispanic American Historical Review*, xi (1931), p. 25.

nitrates. Yet in the face of competition from the synthetic nitrate industry, especially after the war of 1914–18, Chile's share in the world production of nitrates steadily declined. It fell from 73 per cent. in 1894 to 35 per cent. by 1924. Because of the increase in world consumption, this was a relative, not an absolute, decline. But when the full effects of the world economic depression and the collapse of world markets made themselves felt in 1931–2, Chile's share in world production dropped to 11 per cent., and in 1932–3 it was only 5 per cent.[1]

These were the conditions of potential revolution. Already in 1920, in an election comparable in importance to the Argentine election of 1916, a candidate representing the interests of Labour and the middle classes, Arturo Alessandri, the Senator from Tarapacá, had won the Presidency by a narrow margin. But Alessandri's radical programme of reform was, for the most part, frustrated by the opposition of a Conservative Senate, by congressional incompetence, and by administrative inexperience; and when, in 1924, a disillusioned country watched the spectacle of a newly elected Congress failing to approve the budget but, in defiance of the Constitution, voting salaries to its own members, the army entered politics. A military junta imposed itself on the President and its will on Congress, and Alessandri retired into voluntary exile. Recalled as the result of a fresh *coup d'état* four months later, Alessandri now finally discarded the Constitution of 1833, and a new Constitution, ratified by plebiscite, abolished the parliamentary and re-established the presidential system, provided for the direct election of the President, and separated the Church from the State. Hardly had it been promulgated when Alessandri again retired, this time involved in a dispute with his Minister of War, Colonel Carlos Ibáñez, over

[1] Thomson, op. cit., p. 288.

the question of the presidential succession.[1] Ibáñez, the dominant figure in the new administration, was himself elected President in 1927, and from then till 1931 was the virtual dictator of Chile.

The Ibáñez régime was honest (so far as the President was personally concerned), arbitrary, and repressive. It carried into effect most of Alessandri's proposed reforms. It built schools and roads. It greatly expanded the authority of the state. But resting on a basis of military force and lavish expenditure of the public funds, it alienated popular sympathies by its severe restrictions on individual liberty and on the freedom of the press, and it involved the country in financial liabilities far beyond its capacity to meet.[2] In July 1931, caught in the maelstrom of the world depression, which affected Chile more than any other South American country, and as the result of bitter civilian criticism, Ibáñez resigned. A series of *coups d'état* and of transient and embarrassed governments followed. Moderates, radicals, and the military in turn failed to hold office for more than a few months. Not till October 1932, when Alessandri was once more elected to the Presidency by an enormous majority, did Chile return to constitutional government.[3]

Alessandri, however, once regarded as a dangerous radical, was now the hope of the parties of the Right, of the Conservatives and Liberals, who differ mainly in the close alliance between the Conservatives and the Church, and between the Liberals and the newer commercial and in-dustrial aristocracy. The country was restored to stability,

[1] Haring, op. cit., pp. 2–26.

[2] I. J. Cox, in A. C. Wilgus, ed., *Argentina, Brazil and Chile since Independence* (Washington, George Washington Univ. Press, 1935), p. 398, describes Ibáñez as the 'American Mussolini'.

[3] Thomson, op. cit., pp. 283–5; C. H. Haring, 'The Chilean Revolution of 1931', *Hispanic American Historical Review*, xiii (1933), pp. 197–203, and 'Chile Moves Left', *Foreign Affairs*, xvii (April 1939), pp. 618–19.

the budget balanced, the economic crisis conjured away by the ingenious Minister of Finance, Sr. Gustavo Ross. A marked expansion of manufacturing and industry began.[1] Unemployment almost disappeared, and in 1937 a minimum wage law for employees in industry and commerce was enacted. But little was done to promote agrarian reform and, at the end of Alessandri's second administration, the conditions of the urban and rural worker remained far below those obtaining in most civilized countries. Yielding, moreover, to his Conservative supporters, Alessandri adopted a policy of severe repression in his dealings with labour and those new Left-wing groups whose organization accurately reflected the changes in the country's social structure; and it was in the face of this repression that the parties of the Left and Centre—the Communists, the Socialists, the Radical Socialists, the newly created Confederation of Labour, the Democráticos, and the Radicals (a middle-class party which conveniently stretches from Left to Right)—composed in 1936 their numerous differences and combined to establish a Popular Front.[2] In the presidential elections of 1938 the Front chose for its candidate Sr. Pedro Aguirre Cerda, a well-to-do landowner and a prominent educational reformer. An attempted *coup d'état* on behalf of Ibáñez by the so-called Nacista party strengthened its cause, and, in the event, it narrowly defeated the government nominee, Sr. Ross.

This was a new portent in Latin America. But the Popular Front administration did not long survive. It was

[1] See P. T. Ellsworth, *Chile. An Economy in Transition* (New York, Macmillan, 1945), pp. 28–32.
[2] The story is told in J. R. Stevenson, *The Chilean Popular Front* (Philadelphia, Univ. of Pennsylvania Press, 1942). The Communist party, founded in 1921, is the strongest Communist party in Latin America, and contends with the Socialists for control of the Confederation of Labour. The Socialist party was founded in 1931, the C.T.Ch. in 1936.

faced by unprecedented difficulties, caused by a devastating earthquake at the beginning of 1939 and by the outbreak of the second World War at the end. It had to contend with a Liberal and Conservative majority in both Houses of Congress, and it was split by internal dissensions. In 1941 it was replaced by a looser coalition, the Alianza Democrática. In that year also President Aguirre Cerda died. President Juan Antonio Ríos, who defeated Ibáñez in the elections of 1942, was elected on the basis of an even wider coalition than the Popular Front coalition of 1938, is, like his predecessor, a member of the Radical party, and has even less claim to be regarded as a revolutionary.

The reader of *El Diario Ilustrado*, the Conservative organ, or even of *El Mercurio*, the Liberal, might be pardoned, however, for supposing that Chile is on the verge of a social revolution of the most violent kind; and the bitter hostility displayed between the Right- and Left-wing parties is disturbing enough. Even more disturbing, perhaps, is the recrudescence of the old factional irresponsibility. Cabinet crises have been as frequent as in the pre-1924 period. The President has been faced not only with obstruction from Congress (whose budgetary powers were, however, reduced by a constitutional amendment in 1943), but with dictation from the theoretically pro-administration parties, while the parties themselves have tended to fly apart and to re-combine with a vertiginous rapidity. When two or three are gathered together in Chile, there is a political party; when they part, there are at least two more.

The rise of industry has profoundly modified the structure of Chilean society, and there are those who hope that it will form the basis of a new social organization. But the population is small and its purchasing power low. Despite a comprehensive system of social insurance, which owes its inception to Alessandri, disease and malnutrition are widespread, and the rate of infant mortality is one of the highest in the world. Copper and nitrates still dominate the export trade; and the future of nitrates is certainly, and that of copper perhaps, precarious. Agriculture is still the mainstay of more than a third of the working population. But in 1937 less than 1½ per cent. of the rural properties comprised nearly 70 per cent. of the agricultural land.[1] The *hacienda* has outlived its usefulness. But despite the creation in 1928 of a Caja de Colonización Agrícola and the subsequent expansion of its activities, agrarian reform has made little progress; and industrial development without agrarian reform is no answer to the problems of Chile. The strength of the country lies in its genuine devotion to constitutional forms and political principles and the evolutionary development of the democratic process. The stresses and strains in the political, economic, and social fabric are acute. But Chile has so far preferred the path of evolution to that of revolution.

There is a superficial comparison (it is not more than that) between the movement of events in Chile and the movement of events in Mexico. Mexico, like Chile, is an agricultural country dependent for its revenues on mineral exports. The *hacienda* dominated Mexico as it dominated Chile. In both countries the established order of society has been challenged. In both there is a marked trend (not uncommon in Latin America) to policies of nationalization and socialization. But there the comparable ends. Ninetenths of the Mexican people are Indian and mestizo. There has been none of that racial homogeneity and little of that paternalism which have served Chile so well. *Pan, Techo, Abrigo*, 'Bread, Shelter, Cover', was the campaign slogan of the Chilean Popular Front, *Tierra y Libertad,*

[1] Harris, *Economic Problems of Latin America*, p. 307; Soule, Efron, and Ness, *Latin America in the Future World*, p. 75.

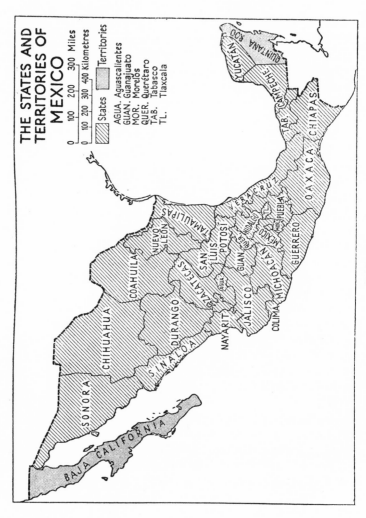

THE STATES AND
TERRITORIES OF
MEXICO

0   100   200   300 Miles
0 100 200 300 400 Kilometres

▧ States   ▢ Territories

AGUA. Aguascalientes
GUAN. Guanajuato
MOR. Morelos
QUER. Querétaro
TAB. Tabasco
TL. Tlaxcala

SONORA
BAJA CALIFORNIA
CHIHUAHUA
SINALOA
DURANGO
COAHUILA
ZACATECAS
NUEVO LEÓN
TAMAULIPAS
NAYARIT
AGUA
SAN LUIS POTOSI
JALISCO
GUAN.
QUER.
HIDALGO
VERACRUZ
COLIMA
MICHOACAN
MEXICO
MOR.
TL.
PUEBLA
GUERRERO
OAXACA
TABASCO
CAMPECHE
YUCATÁN
QUINTANA ROO
CHIAPAS

MAP 12

'Land and Liberty', the cry of the Mexican people; and Mexican history has been a record of violence, not of peaceful change.

Seventy per cent. of the population of Mexico is engaged in agriculture—on the $7\frac{1}{2}$ per cent. of the land that is cultivated.[1] For Mexico, rich in minerals, is poor in land; and the land system is the clue to much, perhaps to most, of Mexican history. The problem is as old as the conquest. In Aztec Mexico the predominant form of land tenure was a primitive Communism, the classic unit the communal village, in which certain plots of land were transmitted from father to son. Yet already the communal village was being engulfed in the private estate, cultivated by peasants bound to the soil. In feudal Spain the great estate was the normal form of landholding, but villages and towns held title to common land—the *ejido*—without their gates. It was easy for these systems to merge. Vast tracts of land, and the villages and Indians upon them, were granted in trust, in *encomiendas*, to the conquerors. But the Spanish Crown recognized also and protected the communal system of landholding. Villages and towns were to have their *ejidos*, and the *ejidos* were not, as in Spain, simply the waste lands at the exit to the village but the whole of its communal agricultural lands.[2]

But of these two main forms of land tenure, the landed estate triumphed at the expense of the landholding village. The *encomiendas* were in time abolished, but not before the *encomenderos* had established a firm control over the Indians and their lands; and the *haciendas*, however acquired, swelled to vast proportions. At the end of the colonial

---

[1] 1930 figures. Simpson, *The Ejido, Mexico's Way Out*, pp. 154, 589.

[2] Simpson, op. cit., pp. 4–14; McBride, *The Land Systems of Mexico*, pp. 111–27; Ernest Gruening, *Mexico and its Heritage* (New York and London Century Co., 1928), pp. 114–17.

period, according to a contemporary estimate, one-fifth of the population owned everything, four-fifths owned nothing. There was at least one property rather larger than Scotland. Not less than a half of the real estate in the country is believed to have been owned by the Church;[1] and though the communal village still existed, the greater part of the Indian and mestizo peasantry was landless and reduced to a state of debt-servitude and peonage.

The establishment of Mexican independence meant, for this landless peasantry, not new freedom but new masters. In Mexico the war of independence began, indeed, as a social revolution. It was to the landless masses that Father Hidalgo appealed in his famous *Grito de Dolores*.[2] But though the Indians and mestizos began the revolution, the creoles completed it, and it was as a Conservative reaction that it ended. Lawyers and intellectuals among the more liberal of the creoles hoped, it is true, to establish a democracy and a republic on the model of the United States.[3] But for the next fifty years Mexican history was a record of tragedy. The population was predominantly illiterate. A large part could not even speak Spanish. The ruling oligarchy was incapable of governing itself. The army was the chief source of power, and revolts, *pronunciamientos*, and barrack-room revolutions were countless. Texas revolted and seceded in 1836, and war with the United States in 1846–8 led to the loss of what are now the states of New Mexico, Arizona, and California. In the middle of the century the rise of a Liberal movement afforded new hope. Like most Latin American Liberal movements, it was anti-clerical; but it had behind it a fund of genuine idealism.

[1] Simpson, op. cit., pp. 17–20; McBride, op. cit., p. 68.
[2] Gruening, op. cit., p. 30.
[3] H. B. Parkes, *A History of Mexico* (London, Methuen, 1938), p. 176.

It has come to be primarily associated with the great name of Benito Juárez, the son of an Indian peasant. Military and clerical privileges were abolished, not before their time. Religious and civil corporations were ordered to divest themselves of their real property, except in so far as this was directly used for civil and religious purposes;[1] and a new Constitution in 1857 attempted to safeguard civil and political rights and specifically forbade civil and ecclesiastical corporations to hold real estate. But the result was to ally the Conservatives, the landowners, the Church (the greatest landlord of all), and the army, yet more determinedly against the Liberals. Civil war followed, in the midst of which Juárez issued still more stringent decrees for the nationalization of all ecclesiastical property and the dissolution of the monasteries. But the country was not only torn by war; it was threatened by foreign intervention, the result of debt default. Spanish troops landed at Vera Cruz in 1861, followed by English and French in 1862; and, after the Spanish and English had withdrawn, Napoleon III erected in Mexico the brief empire of Maximilian of Austria, which survived only till 1867. The French forces were then recalled, the luckless emperor was captured and shot, and Juárez returned to his capital.

Juárez saved the country. Yet it cannot be denied that though the Laws of Reform led to a wider distribution of landownership, the Church lands passed, in the main, into the hands of a new aristocracy, while the prohibition on the ownership of property by civil communities struck a fresh blow at the landowning village. Juárez, moreover, did not live to complete his work; his successor lacked the strength to consolidate it; and in 1876 a *pronunciamiento* by one of Juárez's old lieutenants, Porfirio Díaz, marked the begin-

[1] The Ley Juárez, 1855, and the Ley de Desamortización, or Ley Lerdo, named after Miguel Lerdo de Tejada, 1856.

ning of a new era in Mexican history and of a dictatorship which endured till 1911.

It is not easy to assess the rule of Díaz. Railways, ports, and telegraphs were built. Foreign capital poured into the country. Its shattered finances were restored. Trade spectacularly increased. Banditry was suppressed. Administration became efficient. But Díaz forgot the rock from which he was hewn (he was of part Indian blood); at the end of his régime the mineral wealth, the oil resources, and the industry of the country were, for the most part, in foreign hands; he trained no political class; he did little for the education of his people; and under him the concentration of landownership in a few hands advanced at a prodigious speed. When he fled the country in 1911, nearly three-quarters of the population was illiterate. More than three-quarters lived off the land. Yet 95 per cent. of the rural population was landless. The villages had been shorn of their communal lands. The public domain had been alienated. More than a quarter of the total area of the republic had been sold to a few individuals for a few million dollars; agricultural wages had not risen since 1792; and a high proportion of the Mexican people was in a state of debt-slavery.[1]

The revolution which began in 1910 began as a political movement when Francisco Madero, a wealthy landowner, raised the cry of 'effective suffrage and no re-election'. It ended as a social reformation. Labour wanted relief, the peasant wanted land, and for ten years Mexico passed through the fires of civil war, terrifying, cruel, destructive. In 1917 a new Constitution expressed the aspirations of a new order. There were two famous articles, 27 and 123. Article 27 declared that the ownership of lands, minerals,

[1] Simpson, op. cit., pp. 26–42; McBride, op. cit., pp. 77–81, 154–6; Gruening, op. cit., pp. 136–7.

and waters is vested in the nation, which may grant a title thereto to private persons, thereby constituting private property. Villages deprived of their common lands were to have that land restored, and all villages were given the right to receive lands by outright grant.[1] The size of the great estates was to be limited and title to public land alienated under the Díaz régime to be investigated. Article 123 was in effect an advanced labour code, easier to draft than to apply. Other articles reaffirmed and amplified in an even more stringent form the anti-clerical legislation of the period of the Reform Laws.

The revolutionary programme, put together in somewhat piecemeal form, called for political democracy, popular education, land reform, labour organization, nationalism, and limitations on the power of the Church,[2] which had come to be associated, in Mexico, with reaction. But it was not till 1920 that the work of reconstruction really began, and though Mexico had now begun to move in a spiral rather than a circle,[3] the movement was slow, haphazard, and half-hearted, except perhaps in its recurrent anti-clericalism.[4] Agrarian reform failed to reform. As late as 1930 more than 93 per cent. of the area and more than 90 per cent. of the value of all land in farms was privately owned. Still more remarkable, of this privately owned land more than 83 per cent. was included in less than 3 per cent.

[1] This article embodies the famous decree of 6 January 1915, issued by Venustiano Carranza, of which the immediate effect was to throw the country-side into wild disorder. Simpson, op. cit., p. 54, describes the decree and the article as 'the Magna Carta and fountain-head of the whole legal programme of the agrarian reform' which followed.

[2] C. A. Thomson, 'Mexico's Social Revolution', Foreign Policy Reports, xiii (Aug. 1937), p. 114.

[3] Parkes, op. cit., p. 371.

[4] By 1934 less than 500 priests were permitted to exercise their functions. E. K. James, 'Church and State in Mexico', Foreign Policy Reports, xi (July 1935), p. 111.

of the number of the rural properties. In other words, Mexico was still a land of *haciendas* and *hacendados*.[1] Between 1927 and 1933 the production of basic foodstuffs was less than in the last years of President Díaz, under a system admittedly inefficient.[2] There was, moreover, a genuine division of opinion between those who favoured an extension of the ejidal system of communal agriculture and those who believed that the ultimate aim was to increase the number of small peasant proprietors. Nor was this all. The Labour movement became a prey to division and weakness. The crusade against governmental corruption patently failed. Old revolutionaries, enriched and disillusioned, were now the new Conservatives; and by 1934 the revolution seemed, indeed, to have run its course.[3]

Yet the revolution was now, during the six-year term of President Cárdenas (1934–40), to enter upon its most advanced and active phase. A six-year plan, adopted in 1933, formed the Cárdenas platform. It was couched in vague terms. But it envisaged the reorganization of land-ownership on a co-operative basis, the nationalization of natural resources, an advancing programme of labour legislation, and the reconstruction of the industrial and educational life of the country.[4] By the end of 1940, 47,000,000 acres of land had been distributed to rather more than a million peasants, as compared with some 20,000,000 acres transferred to three-quarters of a million in the previous twenty years.[5] The Government embarked on an extensive programme of agricultural development,

[1] Simpson, op. cit., p. 203; James, *Latin America*, p. 602.
[2] Simpson, op. cit., p. 503.   [3] Thomson, op. cit., p. 114.
[4] See L. L. Lorwin, *National Planning in Selected Countries* (National Resources Planning Board, Technical Paper No. 2, Washington, Government Printing Office, 1941), p. 122; C. A. Thomson, 'Mexico's Challenge to Foreign Capital', *Foreign Policy Reports*, xiii (Aug. 1937), p. 126.
[5] James, *Latin America*, p. 602.

rural education, and public works. In certain areas, such as La Laguna, it attempted to reorganize the economic and social basis of an entire region.[1] The Labour movement was revived and the Confederation of Mexican Workers organized in 1936 on a basis of industrial unionism; while the trend towards the creation of a more independent economy and the strengthening of national sovereignty by national control over natural resources was spectacularly illustrated by the expropriation of the foreign oil companies in March 1938.

So ambitious a programme of social and economic regeneration inevitably caused immense difficulties. Labour problems were acute. Agriculture was disorganized. The Government's methods provoked violent hostility outside Mexico as well as bitterness within it. The President himself was virtually a dictator, resting for support on the workers, the peasants, and the army, who, together with the civil servants, formed the reorganized Party of the Mexican Revolution. But President Cárdenas's dictatorship was a dictatorship unprecedented in Mexican history, not only in the President's personal devotion to an ideal, but in his tolerance of criticism. It was, moreover, of great importance that in 1940 the principle of 'no re-election'—a principle more familiar in Mexican theory than in Mexican practice—should have been put into operation, when President Cárdenas quietly surrendered his powers to his successor, President Avila Camacho.

Since the new President was the choice of the Party of the Mexican Revolution and of General Cárdenas himself, it was almost inevitable that he should have been elected. There was no abrupt break with the immediate past, no

---

[1] Thomson, *Foreign Policy Reports*, xiii. 129; Clarence Senior, 'The Laguna Region—Mexico's Agrarian Laboratory', *Quarterly Journal of Inter-American Relations*, i (Oct. 1939), pp. 67–78.

sudden reversal of the policies pursued by the previous régime. But under President Avila Camacho the Mexican revolution entered yet another phase—the phase of consolidation. Further reforms were introduced into the land laws, with the intent of protecting the smallholder and of giving the peasant definite title to land. There were reforms in the Labour Laws, reforms in the Government Party (from which the military were now excluded), and reforms in the Constitution (granting to the judges of the Supreme Court, for example, tenure for life); and more than any previous government the Government of President Avila Camacho deserved to be called a Government of national unity.

The Mexican revolution was the product of Mexican history and Mexican conditions. It has penetrated deeply into the structure of Mexican life. It has given to Mexicans not a new land but a new hope; and whatever régime may succeed in Mexico, it cannot ignore the new aspirations that have been released. This is not government by the people, but it is to a large extent government for the people. The difficulties yet to be overcome are enormous. The problem of bureaucratic efficiency has not been solved. The economic foundations of the state are still precarious. The more Liberal programme of President Avila Camacho has not lessened the wide gulf which is still fixed between Left and Right, and there are aspects of the revolutionary programme and of the attitude both of the Right wing and of the Left which are deeply disturbing. But the Mexican revolution, whatever may be thought of it, is the most significant phenomenon in the modern history of Latin America. What is remarkable is not that it has achieved so little but that it has achieved so much.

VII

HEMISPHERE RELATIONS

IT is customary to think of the Latin American states as a family united both by history and geography. But in the nineteenth century the forces of isolation, of separatism, and of disunity were stronger in Latin America than the forces of unity.[1] Bolívar had dreamed of a Latin, or at least a Spanish American League of Nations. He had seen in the isthmus of Panamá the future capital of the world.[2] But the Panamá Congress of 1826, which was designed to lay the foundation for the realization of these ideals, was a failure, except in so far as it afforded an inspiration for a distant future. The new states differed in size and strength. Their frontiers were ill defined and almost invariably disputed.[3] Internal disorders as well as external ambitions fostered international strife. In Central America the brief trial of federation only served to plunge that turbulent area into conflict. In South America Uruguay was for long a battlefield between Argentina and Brazil. Paraguay, emerging from her Tibetan isolation, aspired to play the part of a South American Prussia. Chile's expansion on the Pacific was made at the expense of Peru and Bolivia.

[1] Quincy Wright, 'The Historic Circumstances of Enduring Peace', in S. Pargellis, ed., *The Quest for Political Unity in World History* (American Historical Association, *Annual Report*, 1942, vol. iii, Washington, Government Printing Office, 1944), p. 365, points out that in the century between 1815 and 1914 there was more loss of life by war and civil war in North and South America than in Europe.

[2] J. B. Scott, ed., *The International Conferences of American States, 1889–1928* (New York, Carnegie Endowment, 1931), pp. xix–xxix.

[3] See Gordon Ireland, *Boundaries, Possessions, and Conflicts in South America* (Harvard Univ. Press, 1938), and *Boundaries, Possessions, and Conflicts in Central and North America and the Caribbean* (ibid., 1941).

Peru, in the bitterness of defeat, sought compensation in Amazon adventures which brought her into conflict with Colombia and Ecuador; and the claustrophobia of Bolivia, shorn of her Pacific coastline, directly led, in more recent times, to war with Paraguay.[1]

It followed that for the greater part of the nineteenth century such political relations as existed between the majority of the Latin American states tended to be un-friendly. Geography forbade that they should be intimate; and both intellectually and economically the new states were linked more closely to Europe than to one another. Even in 1938 less than one-tenth of the total trade of the Latin American area took place between the Latin American countries themselves.[2] All the Spanish American republics, moreover, had to attain some degree of order and coherence before any effective co-operation between them could be expected. Yet the Bolivarian ideal of unity and solidarity, reinforced by fears of Europe or the United States, never wholly died. It was reflected in more than one attempt to hold an inter-state Congress; and the Latin American countries boast, in their quest for peace and con-cord, of a long and honourable record of the peaceful settlement of disputes.[3] Since 1870, indeed, neither of the two greatest of the South American states, Argentina and Brazil, has ever resorted to war within the continent, and

[1] The five greater wars of South America were Argentina and Brazil, 1825–8; Argentina against Uruguay and ultimately Brazil, 1842–52; Paraguay against Argentina, Uruguay, and Brazil, 1864–70; Chile against Peru and Bolivia, 1879–83; Bolivia and Paraguay, 1932–5.

[2] See *Inter-American Statistical Yearbook, 1942* (ed. R. C. Migone, New York, Macmillan, 1942), p. 173.

[3] The proposal to substitute conciliation or mediation for the arbitra-ment of war in inter-American affairs goes back to the Panamá Congress of 1826. The Latin American states are apt, indeed, to regard themselves as the discoverers and, as it were, patentees, of conciliation and arbitration procedure.

the continental influence of Brazil, in particular, has been almost wholly pacific.

In the age of the telephone, the radio, and the aeroplane, it is still true that the political and economic relations between the Latin American countries as a whole are neither uniformly close nor uniformly friendly. As late as 1941 Peru and Ecuador resorted to arms. The rising forces of nationalism in Latin America, supported by greater economic strength and more powerful armaments, may yet take an aggressive turn, and the weakness of the two land-locked states, Bolivia and Paraguay, may yet prove to be a source of danger not only to themselves but to the peace of the continent. But while the conditions of the nineteenth century made for isolation and disunity, those of the twentieth century make for closer association. The physical obstacles between the Latin American countries are now less formidable. The gradual diversification of the Latin American economies favours the prospects of increased commercial interchange. In international affairs the tendency of the twenty republics to join together as a bloc in support of what they conceive to be their primary and mutual interests has long been marked; and, politically, all are joined with the United States in the regional organization for peace and security known as the Pan American system. The attitude of the Latin American states towards the United States is, indeed, strangely compounded of attraction and repulsion. But it is within the institutions of the Union of American Republics and the framework of Pan Americanism that the relations of the Latin American countries, not only with the United States but between themselves, have grown more intimate and more harmonious.

Only with one Latin American state, Mexico, has the United States ever been formally at war, though that war, an incident in the imperial sweep of the United States from the Atlantic to the Pacific, cost Mexico half of her national territory. In Central America and the Caribbean the United States intervened repeatedly and by force of arms in the first quarter of the present century. But in South America it has never subjected any state to such threats of force as Argentina suffered from Great Britain and France in 1845[1] or Venezuela from Germany in 1902, although the United States came near to war with Chile in 1891–2,[2] and while its relations with Brazil have been almost consistently cordial, with Argentina they have been as consistently cool.

These differences are sufficiently striking; but they are differences within a larger pattern of behaviour, a distinctively Latin American policy of the United States. In 1822 the United States was the first Power to recognize the independence of any Latin American state. In December 1823, when the Monroe Doctrine was formulated, it held up a hand in warning to Europe.

'With the Governments who have declared their independence and maintained it, and whose independence we have, on great consideration and on just principles, acknowledged'— so ran President Monroe's message to Congress—'we could not view any interposition for the purpose of oppressing them, or controlling in any other manner their destiny, by any European power in any other light than as a manifestation of an unfriendly disposition towards the United States.'

The Monroe Doctrine was—it still is—a prohibition by the United States against the extension of European power

---

[1] See J. F. Cady, *Foreign Intervention in the Rio de la Plata, 1828–50* (Philadelphia, Univ. of Pennsylvania Press, 1929).

[2] Osgood Hardy, 'The Itata Incident', *Hispanic American Historical Review*, v (1922), pp. 195–226; H. C. Evans, *Chile and Its Relations with the United States* (Durham, N. C., Duke Univ. Press, 1927), pp. 135–54.

and influence in the New World.[1] It was, in origin, partly an expression of a 'good neighbour' policy, a generous gesture of sympathy on behalf of the Latin American peoples still struggling to be free. It was partly a measure of national security; and it was partly designed to establish the political pre-eminence of the United States within the western hemisphere, and thus also to secure its economic interests. It expressed two fundamental beliefs: first that a 'political system' existed in the New World different from that of the Old, and secondly, that the extension of the power and influence of the Old World in the New would endanger the safety of the United States itself.

It does not matter that in December 1823 the danger of European intervention in Latin America was remote, or that, in the nineteenth century, not the Monroe Doctrine but the British fleet stood between Latin America and Europe.[2] Nor is it of vital concern to decide what part of the famous message was dictated by the mild Monroe himself and what by the energetic John Quincy Adams, loath to see the United States as 'a cock-boat in the wake of the British man-of-war'. What is important is that the ideas which Monroe expressed were American sentiments and American principles. The Monroe Doctrine grew with the growth of the American nation; the hand held out in warning to Europe grew larger, not smaller; and the principles enunciated in 1823 became the standards and maxims of American foreign policy. They still prevail to-day.

It is true that during a major part of the nineteenth century the Monroe Doctrine was neither consistently nor rigorously applied. The United States was principally con-

[1] Dexter Perkins, *Hands Off. A History of the Monroe Doctrine* (Boston, Little, Brown, 1943), p. 4. In this book Professor Perkins summarizes the results of his more detailed studies of the Monroe Doctrine and continues them on a less intensive scale. It is by far the best single volume on a subject on which much has been written. [2] *Ante*, pp. 47, 50.

cerned with the exploration, occupation, and exploitation of the North American continent. It displayed little interest in political co-operation with its southern neighbours. The principles of 1823 were, from time to time, reaffirmed and even expanded. They were, on occasion, invoked and vindicated.[1] They acquired the status of a tradition. But they were also violated,[2] and it was not till the last decade of the century that they were proclaimed with a vigour which initiated a new stage not only in the history of the Monroe Doctrine itself but in the Latin American policy of the United States.

By the eighteen-nineties the process of the exploration and occupation of the North American continent was practically complete. American industry had developed to the point at which it needed foreign markets. American capital looked abroad; and the frontiers of the United States were now to be pushed out westwards into the Pacific and southwards into the Caribbean. This was the beginning of a revolution in the position of the United States as a world power, and with that revolution the Monroe Doctrine experienced a remarkable extension. No longer merely protective and mainly passive, it now became both active and aggressive. 'Today', wrote Secretary of State Olney in a famous dispatch, addressed to Great Britain, in 1895, 'the United States is practically sovereign on this continent, and its fiat is law upon the subjects to which it confines its interposition . . .';[3] and for Latin America as well as Europe the signs were plain for all to read. In 1901 the United States acquired the right

[1] In opposition, for example, to French intervention in Mexico during and after the American Civil War and to Spanish resumption of sovereignty over Santo Domingo from 1861 to 1865.

[2] Thus Great Britain and France jointly blockaded the Río de la Plata in 1845 and Spain temporarily occupied the Chincha islands off the coast of Peru in 1864.   [3] Perkins, op. cit., p. 175.

to intervene in Cuba, newly liberated from Spain, to preserve domestic order and national 'independence'. Two
years later, President Theodore Roosevelt, faced with
Colombian opposition to his plans for a Panamá Canal,
took three weeks to assist at the birth of the Panamá republic,
to recognize the new state, and to sign a treaty under which
the United States acquired quasi-sovereign rights over the
canal zone;[1] and in 1904, in his annual message to Congress, the President formulated what has come to be known
as the 'Roosevelt corollary' to the Monroe Doctrine.
Chronic wrongdoing or the lack of order in any country, he
declared, called for the intervention of civilized states, 'and
in the western hemisphere the adherence of the United
States to the Monroe Doctrine may force the United States,
however reluctantly, in flagrant cases of such wrongdoing
or impotence, to the exercise of an international police
power'.[2]

Within the next twenty-five years the United States
intervened repeatedly in the affairs of the smaller states
of Central America and the Caribbean area.[3] It formed
an American Provisional Government in Cuba between
1906 and 1909. American military and fiscal control was
established in Haiti and the Dominican Republic. In
Central America the United States declined to recognize
revolutionary governments established by force—a procedure denounced in Latin America as 'diplomatic intervention'—and it made use of varying forms of political
and economic pressure. American marines were landed in
Nicaragua in 1912 and remained there with a brief interval

[1] W. D. McCain, *The United States and the Republic of Panamá* (Durham,
N. C., Duke Univ. Press, 1937), pp. 14–17.
[2] H. C. Hill, *Roosevelt and the Caribbean* (Univ. of Chicago Press, 1927),
p. 149.
[3] D. G. Munro, *The United States and the Caribbean Area* (Boston, World
Peace Foundation, 1934), is the best short comprehensive treatment.

till 1933, and the United States intervened by force of arms in Mexico in 1914 and again in 1916–17.

The purposes and motives for these repeated interventions varied. The United States followed in the Caribbean area no planned and predetermined policy. In part the prohibition upon European intervention in the western hemisphere itself obliged the United States to intervene to protect not only its own interests but, in some measure also, those of the European Powers, when these interests and property rights were threatened by maladministration, robbery, or disorder. The Roosevelt corollary thus received, for example, the support of Great Britain in a way in which Britain had never previously accepted the full interpretation of the original Monroe Doctrine. In part, there was an imperial sense of 'manifest destiny'. President Roosevelt's view of Kipling's *The White Man's Burden* is well known. 'Rather poor poetry', he commented, 'but good sense from the expansion standpoint.'[1] But, above all, the new policy reflected the strategic and economic interests of the United States. The acquisition of the Panamá Canal Zone had greatly increased the strategic importance of the Caribbean area to the United States. United States commerce in that area phenomenally increased, and when President Taft explained that United States diplomacy might well be made to 'include active intervention to secure for our merchandise and our capitalists opportunity for profitable investment',[2] 'dollar diplomacy' came into its own.

But the third constant element in United States policy, the ideological element, was also present. It was apparent both in American efforts to promote peace in Central

[1] Hill, op. cit., p. 204.
[2] J. W. Garner, *American Foreign Policies* (New York Univ. Press, 1928), p. 39.

America, and in President Wilson's belief that he could 'teach the South American republics to elect good men';[1] and, while, in the first quarter of the twentieth century, the principles of the Monroe Doctrine were still farther developed against European, and indeed Asiatic, expansion in the western hemisphere, the interventionist activities of the United States did not extend beyond the Caribbean. They reflected a Caribbean rather than a Latin American policy of the United States; and, given the enormous disparity in power and resources between the United States and the Caribbean states, the United States employed its coercive powers with remarkable moderation and often with reluctance.

Even the original Monroe Doctrine, however, had never achieved more than a transient popularity in Latin America. Already in 1824 the first flush of enthusiasm which it evoked rapidly paled. One or another of the Latin American states had from time to time found it convenient to appeal to the principles on which it was founded. But even when such an appeal was answered, the gratitude that resulted was short-lived, and, with the twentieth-century extension of the doctrine, scepticism or indifference turned into positive hostility. For motives that were commercial rather than political the United States had initiated in 1889 the first Pan American Conference (at which all the American states except Canada and the Dominican Republic were present), and this conference was responsible for the establishment of the International Union of American Republics, or, as it later became, the Union of American Republics. But though this early Pan American movement reflected the growing interest of the United States in the peaceful development of the hemisphere, it

[1] B. J. Hendrick, *The Life and Letters of Walter H. Page* (2 vols., New York, Doubleday, Page, 1925), i. 204.

did little to promote political solidarity, and both before and after the war of 1914–18 the spirit of distrust was amply evident. It was notable that though twelve of the Latin American republics followed the United States into war in 1917–18 or severed relations with the Central Powers, three of the four leading countries, Argentina, Chile, and Mexico, and two of the most important Caribbean republics, Colombia and Venezuela, remained neutral.[1] After the war the United States stood aloof from the League of Nations, but most of the Latin American states were original members; and, in that hopeful dawn, the League not only strongly appealed to the genuine idealism of the Latin American mind; what was equally cogent, it appeared to provide a counterpoise to the power and influence of the United States.[2] It was, then, to Geneva, not to Washington, that the Latin American states momentarily looked; and when, indeed, in 1928, the sixth Pan American Conference met at Havana, so bitter were the feelings then displayed towards the United States and so evident the resentment both at United States commercial policy and at United States intervention in the Caribbean that the conference seemed to portend the dissolution of the Pan American movement itself.[3]

But the Havana Conference, with the realization on the part of the United States of the increasing hostility of the Latin American countries and its own diminishing influence, opened a new period in the history of Pan Americanism. Already there had been signs of a retreat from the expanded interpretation of the Monroe Doctrine current in

---

[1] Perkins, op. cit., p. 325.   [2] See below, pp. 171–2.

[3] It threatened, wrote the future President Roosevelt in an article on 'Our Foreign Policy: a Democratic View', in *Foreign Affairs*, vi (July 1928), p. 585, 'to bring out not only hostile speeches but definitely hostile action towards the United States'. See also John P. Humphrey, *The Inter-American System. A Canadian View* (Toronto, Macmillan, 1942), p. 92.

the early years of the century. It had been anticipated by
President Wilson. In a famous speech at Mobile in 1913
Wilson had endeavoured to reassure the Latin American
states that the United States would 'never seek one additional foot of territory by conquest'.[1] He repudiated
'dollar diplomacy'. If, he said, American enterprise imposed on or exploited the people of another country, 'it
ought to be checked and not encouraged'.[2] But with a high
moral fervour, Wilson believed that it was possible to impose democracy by force, and partly by reason of this
belief, partly in the grip of circumstance, he was led to
continue the interventionist policy of his predecessors.
After the war of 1914–18, Secretary Hughes similarly tried
to reassure the Latin American states, and it was Hughes
who was responsible for the withdrawal of American troops
from the Dominican Republic in 1924 and from Nicaragua
in 1925. But these gestures were obscured by fresh intervention in Nicaragua in 1926; and though, in 1927, the
appointment of Mr. Dwight Morrow as Ambassador to
Mexico began an improvement in United States–Mexican
relations, it was the year 1928 that marked the all-important change.

The Havana Conference met in January. In December
a famous State Department memorandum, the Clark
Memorandum, repudiated in explicit terms the 'Roosevelt
corollary'.[3] Two years later the memorandum was made
public. Thenceforth the Monroe Doctrine was restored to
something like its original meaning, as a doctrine which,
in the words of the Clark Memorandum, states a case of the
United States versus Europe, not of the United States
versus Latin America. The United States had not, indeed,

---

[1] Perkins, op. cit., p. 323.   [2] Garner, op. cit., p. 41.
[3] S. F. Bemis, *The Latin American Policy of the United States* (New York,
Harcourt, Brace, 1943), p. 221.

renounced the right of intervention in Latin America, but it no longer based that right on the principles of 1823;[1] and though a decisive change in United States policy was thus initiated under the Republican administrations of Presidents Coolidge and Hoover, it remained for President Franklin Roosevelt to transform the negative process of withdrawal from interventionist diplomacy into the positive process of actively seeking the co-operation of the Latin American states in the affairs of the western hemisphere. The proclamation of the 'Good Neighbour' policy in 1933 was more than a realization that the Caribbean policy of the United States had outlived its usefulness and was in fact menacing the political and economic relations of the United States with the Latin American states. It was an expression of American idealism at its best, and it was a recognition also of the increasing maturity of the Latin American states.

If, from one point of view, this new policy represented a natural evolution of tendencies which had already appeared under the Hoover administration, in another it was a definite break with the past. The Monroe Doctrine was certainly not abandoned. But the 'Good Neighbour' policy not only involved the renunciation by the United States of the right of intervention in the affairs of its nearer neighbours, the recognition of *de facto* governments in Latin America, and the abandonment of the functions of the United States Government as a debt-collecting agency on behalf of its own or European nationals; it meant acceptance of the principle of collaboration and consultation between the American nations in all matters of common concern.

On the negative side the process of liquidating the previous Caribbean policy of the United States was com-

[1] Perkins, op. cit., p. 344.

pleted by the removal of American marines from Haiti in 1934, the surrender, in the same year, of the right to intervene in Cuba, the negotiation in 1936 of a new treaty with Panamá, under which the United States surrendered its right to intervene in that small state also, and the relinquishment in 1940 of American control of the Dominican customs. Haiti has still not attained to complete financial independence, and in Cuba the United States still maintains, on a reciprocal basis, special economic privileges in the shape of preferential tariff treatment.

The positive side of the new programme was reflected at successive Pan American Conferences. The seventh Pan American Conference at Montevideo in 1933, at which the United States accepted a resolution denying the right of intervention by one state in the internal or external affairs of another, infused new life into the Pan American movement. Three years later, at Buenos Aires, the Inter-American Conference for the Maintenance of Peace, opened by President Roosevelt in person, adopted a still more sweeping protocol against the right and practice of intervention. Its consultative pact recognized also the joint responsibility of the American nations to prevent hostilities between themselves and provided for consultation in the event of a threat to the peace of the hemisphere from within or without its borders. In 1938, at the eighth Pan American Conference at Lima, these pledges were renewed in more specific form and machinery was now devised to implement the procedure of consultation agreed upon at Buenos Aires. Meanwhile, the more liberal trading policy of the United States, initiated by Mr. Cordell Hull under the Reciprocal Trade Agreements Act of 1934, had found in Latin America its most effective sphere of operation, and by the end of 1939 agreements had been concluded with eleven Latin American states.

These advances were not, it is true, accepted by the Latin American states uncritically. At the Buenos Aires Conference of 1936 an attempt on the part of the United States to impose its neutrality legislation on the Pan American system was defeated.[1] Argentina, always resentful of United States leadership, cultivated a role of lofty independence. At the Buenos Aires Conference the Argentine delegation resolutely opposed a United States proposal to establish permanent machinery of inter-American consultation.[2] At the time of the Lima Conference the Argentine Foreign Minister not only proceeded to Lima by battleship, but retired to the Chilean lakes three days after the conference had begun. But even with Argentina United States relations were far more cordial in 1939 than in 1933. The restraint exercised by the United States in its dealings with Mexico, after the expropriation of the foreign oil companies, in 1938, was a further sign of the changed temper of the times; and by 1939, indeed, far closer and more genuinely co-operative relations had been established between the American republics than at any time in their history. The sphere and scope of the Pan American movement had been widened and the Monroe Doctrine itself had been given a basis of continental support. The contrast now was not between the bright hopes of the League of Nations and the halting progress of the Pan American movement, but between the failing vitality of the League and a Pan American movement infused with new vigour. To the Latin American states the very failure of the universal League pointed the attractions of the regional Pan American system, while the gathering clouds over Europe intensified the efforts of the United States to establish in the Americas a genuinely co-operative system

---

[1] C. G. Fenwick, 'The Buenos Aires Conference: 1936', *Foreign Policy Reports*, viii (July 1937), pp. 95–6.   [2] Bemis, op. cit., p. 287.

with common action for defence. Once again the Latin American policy of the United States reflected, as it had always reflected, a mixture of self-interest and idealism. It was properly concerned with considerations of political security and economic advantage, but it illustrated also that idealism which had failed in its larger hopes in the nineteen-twenties. From this point of view the 'Good Neighbour' policy was the true heir of Wilsonian idealism.

The Pan American system, thus revitalized in the nineteen-thirties, is, of course, neither Pan American nor a system, in the exact meaning of those words.[1] It does not include Canada, or the colonies and possessions of the European Powers in the Americas. It has had no centralized administration, no written Constitution similar to the old Covenant of the League, no Council, no Assembly, no Permanent Court. Only a few of its organs rest on formal conventions. The Union of American Republics is an entirely voluntary association of theoretically equal sovereign states. It maintains in Washington a permanent bureau, the Pan American Union, which is an organization of research and propaganda as well as the permanent secretariat of the central institution of the Union, the International Conferences of American States. It maintains also a large number of specialized offices, committees, and commissions, some of which are now concerned with the broadest problems of political, economic, and social policy in the Americas; and the pattern of inter-American organization is completed by an elaborate network of declarations, resolutions, and conventions designed to ensure the preservation of peace in the western hemisphere. Eight full conferences of the American states have been held, besides

[1] For descriptions see Humphrey, op. cit., and M. M. Ball, *The Problem of Inter-American Organisation* (Stanford Univ. Press, 1944).

a great variety of special and technical conferences, since 1889.

There are obvious lacunae in this regional framework. The machinery for the pacific settlement of disputes fails to include provisions for defining an aggressor,[1] and it was not till 1945, at the Inter-American Conference on Problems of War and Peace at Mexico City, that arrangements were made for applying sanctions. The Union has no coercive authority. Its decisions are not binding on states-members. The resolutions and recommendations of the Pan American Conferences require the ratification of the states concerned, and many of them, indeed, remain no more than pious aspirations. By 1943, for example, Argentina had ratified only six out of ninety Pan American conventions concluded since 1890.[2] But the Union has shown an extraordinary adaptability to changing circumstances, and its services to the peace and welfare of the western hemisphere are indisputable.

The outbreak of war in 1939 naturally strengthened this system of inter-American co-operation and consultation. On the one hand, the Latin American countries turned to the United States for economic and financial support; on the other, the United States sought to bring all the American republics to act together both in strategy and policy. Within three weeks of the beginning of the war the American Foreign Ministers met, for the first time in history, at Panamá, in accordance with the consultative machinery devised at Lima in 1938.[3] They there agreed to establish a

---

[1] Nor has it always prevented war or the threat of war. In the Bolivian-Paraguayan dispute (1932–5) the only pacific settlement treaty to which both countries were parties was the Covenant of the League of Nations, and the Leticia dispute between Peru and Colombia (1932–4) was settled by League intervention.   [2] Bemis, op. cit., p. 261.

[3] Developments since 1939 may most conveniently be followed in the *Reports* of the Foreign Policy Association, in the accounts of conferences

'neutrality zone' round the western hemisphere, created an Inter-American Neutrality Committee, and, most important of all, established an Inter-American Financial and Economic Advisory Committee, which was designed to reduce the economic consequences of the war in Latin America. They met again at Havana in 1940. The emphasis had now shifted from neutrality to defence. At Havana machinery was devised for taking over, in case of need, the administration of European colonies in the western hemisphere. The Convention on the Provisional Administration of European Colonies and Possessions in the Americas not only placed on a Pan American basis that part of the Monroe Doctrine which prohibits the transfer of American territory from one non-American Power to another; it asserted a right of control over those colonies if the sovereignty of the mother country was materially impaired. Finally, the resolution of the Havana Conference, that any attack by a non-American state against the integrity of an American state would be considered as an act of aggression against all, brought the American republics perceptibly nearer towards the establishment of a genuine system of regional security.

The third meeting of American Foreign Ministers took place at Rio de Janeiro in 1942, after that act of aggression had been committed. The six Central American and the three island republics had followed the United States into war; Mexico, Colombia, and Venezuela had severed relations with the Axis Powers; and the remaining states of South America had either undertaken to treat the United States as though she were non-belligerent, or had formally declared their solidarity with her. The Rio Conference

published in *International Conciliation*, by the Carnegie Endowment for International Peace, and in the annual volume, *Inter-American Affairs* (ed. A. P. Whitaker, Columbia Univ. Press, 1942-).

provided for fresh machinery—an Inter-American Defence Board, an Emergency Advisory Committee for Political Defence—to safeguard the strategic interests of the western hemisphere. Its elaborate economic arrangements committed the American republics to a policy of full economic collaboration during the war and looked towards continued co-operation after it. Its recommendations that all the American republics should sever diplomatic and commercial relations with the Axis Powers were major political decisions. When the conference closed only Argentina and Chile remained in relations with the Axis, and within a few months, in May and August 1942, both Mexico and Brazil entered the war.

Yet the recommendation in favour of a severance of relations with the Axis Powers had only been passed at Rio de Janeiro (and that in a much weakened form) after a severe struggle in which Argentina had played the leading role. It was not till January 1943 that Chile severed such relations and not till January 1944 that Argentina took the same action; and when in January 1945 the American Foreign Ministers met, for the fourth time, at Mexico City to discuss the problems of war and peace, Argentina was not present. The United States, indeed, and most of the Latin American countries were no longer in normal relations with the Argentine Government, and between the United States and Argentina relations were deeply and unprecedentedly embittered.

The Mexico City Conference, however, opened a door to reconciliation between Argentina and the sister-republics, and, ostensibly at least, that reconciliation took place when Argentina adhered to its final act; and while the resolutions and recommendations of the Mexico City Conference envisaged the systematization of the agencies and the strengthening of the authority of the inter-American system, the Act of Chapultepec still further placed the Monroe Doctrine upon a regional basis. It still remains a United States doctrine. But it has been buttressed as never before by continental support. The Act of Chapultepec not only declared that an act of aggression against an American state should be considered as an aggression against all American states; it made it clear that this definition included aggression by one American state against another. This was sufficiently remarkable. But the Act went farther. It took some steps to define an aggressor; it provided sanctions, including, ultimately, the use of armed force; and while it committed the American states to the application of such sanctions while the war continued, it looked also towards the conclusion after the war of a treaty which would impose this obligation in permanent and binding form.

Since 1939, then, the political relations between the American republics have become far closer knit. In view of the old legacy of suspicion left by the Caribbean policy of the United States in Latin America, the facts that by joint agreement United States bases were permitted to be established in Latin American territory, and that joint-defence boards were formed with Mexico and Brazil, were little short of revolutionary; and while United States trade with Latin America naturally increased and the United States launched a broad programme of practical aid to the Latin American states, in economic affairs the 'Good Neighbour' policy spoke in the benevolent language of a New Deal for the Americas. The United States sought not only to mobilize the resources of the hemisphere for the purposes of war, but to rebuild the Latin American economies for the pursuits of peace. It was increasingly concerned with the economic development of its neighbours.[1]

[1] See Humphreys, 'Latin America and the Post-War World', *Agenda*, ii (1943), pp. 80–92.

This is a policy of enlightened self-interest, based as much on permanent political and strategic interests as on commercial considerations and temporary necessities. But it would be easy to exaggerate the degree of integration that has been or can be achieved or the extent to which old suspicions have been overcome. No partial grouping of the Latin American states, the so-called southern bloc, or a northern Bolivian bloc, has ever become clearly or precisely defined. The Pan American movement has not been effectively threatened from within the hemisphere. Yet great unresolved problems still remain in the relations between the United States and the Latin American states, and whatever the degree of partnership attained between the American peoples, political, economic, and indeed psychological facts forbid that it can ever be a partnership in isolation. While the Old World needs the assistance of the New, the New World, in the words of Mr. Sumner Welles, 'can never attain that measure of security and well-being to which it aspires except in collaboration' with other states and other regions. The problems of the New World and the problems of the Old are interdependent. They cannot be solved apart.

VIII

LATIN AMERICA IN WORLD AFFAIRS

THE illusion that the Americas form a continental unit,
distinct and separate from the rest of the world, has
been dangerous and persistent. It is true that the western
hemisphere is a continental island, and that North and
South America are connected by land. But, as yet, no one
crosses the isthmus of Panamá, except from sea to sea. The
whole of South America, and much of Central America as
well, are overseas to the United States. By air, Washington
is nearer to Moscow than to Buenos Aires, and Rio de
Janeiro is more distant from the centre of the North
American continent than any European capital except
Athens; by sea, Gibraltar is closer to the South Atlantic
coast of South America than is the nearest point in the
United States, and European bases on the coast of Africa
are nearer to southern South America than are United
States bases in the Caribbean. The South Atlantic is a
uniting rather than a dividing element in world affairs. If,
for the purposes of defence, the western hemisphere is a
single unit, the lines of that defence stretch far beyond its
continental boundaries.[1]

While the western hemisphere is not strategically self-
contained, neither is it, nor is it likely to become, economically self-contained. The dependence of the Latin American
countries on the markets of the United States decreases from
north to south, and their dependence on Europe increases
proportionately. Three groups of countries may be distinguished, on the basis of production and trade. There is,

---

[1] Cf. Eugene Staley, 'The Myth of the Continents', *Foreign Affairs*, xix
(April 1941), pp. 481–94, revised and reissued in H. W. Weigert and V.
Stefansson, *Compass of the World* (New York, Macmillan, 1944), pp. 89–108.

MAP 13

THE WORLD RELATIONSHIPS OF LATIN AMERICA

Azimuthal Equidistant Projection centred on Washington, D.C.
On this map, the straight line connecting Washington with any
other point on the globe is a great circle, which is the shortest
distance between these two points. All distances measured along
great circle routes from Washington are true distances and are
therefore directly comparable.

first, a Caribbean group, whose trade is closely integrated with that of the United States, and whose products are mostly not competitive with United States products. Secondly, there is what may be termed an Andean group, consisting of Bolivia, Peru, and Ecuador, whose trade has been roughly divided between the United States and Europe. Thirdly, there is a southern group, comprising Argentina, Brazil, Uruguay, Paraguay, and Chile, whose products are, for the most part, either directly competitive with United States products or, where they are not competitive, are produced in excess of United States demand.

This division is, of course, an extremely rough one, and in each group there are particular variations which modify, though they do not invalidate, the general statement. The fact remains that Argentina, Uruguay, Brazil, and Chile have generally accounted for more than half the total export trade of Latin America; and in 1938, though the United States took one-third of the exports of Brazil, it absorbed less than a sixth of those of Chile, less than a tenth of those of Argentina, and only 4 per cent. of those of Uruguay.[1] In normal times some two-fifths of Latin American exports have been sold within the hemisphere and three-fifths outside it.[2]

It is true that the gradual diversification of the Latin American economies, and the spread of industrialization, will permanently improve the prospects of inter-American trade, as well as of trade between the Latin American

[1] See Alvin H. Hansen, 'Hemisphere Solidarity', *Foreign Affairs*, xix (Oct. 1940), pp. 12–21, and P. W. Bidwell, *Economic Defense of Latin America* (Boston, World Peace Foundation, 1941), p. 13. Latin American trade figures are conveniently assembled in *The Foreign Trade of Latin America* (United States Tariff Commission, revised, 3 parts in 4 vols., Report No. 146, Second Series, Washington, 1942).

[2] Before the war the hemisphere as a whole bought $3,200 million worth of goods outside it and sold $4,100 million worth outside it. Bidwell, op. cit., pp. 85–6.

countries themselves. It is true, also, that the effects of war
have been to bind together the economic life of the Americas
more closely than ever before. During the war the United
States became the chief source of supply and the chief
market of all the Latin American states, except Argentina;
and however much this condition may be modified, fresh
grooves have been cut in the pattern of inter-American
economic life and new lines of development accentuated.[1]
Yet, for the western hemisphere, the achievement of
economic equilibrium in isolation from other parts of the
world would be a task of enormous difficulty. Even if its
trade were so rearranged as to secure the nearest possible
approach to hemispheric self-sufficiency, no adequate outlet for most of the principal South American agricultural
and pastoral products could be found within the hemisphere. In the future, as in the past, Britain and continental
Europe must provide for the southern Latin American
states those markets which the United States cannot provide, except at the cost of grave distress to its own primary
producers. Plans for hemispheric self-sufficiency, at one
time current in the United States, were counsels of despair,
based on the assumption of a world organized for war, not
for peace.

While, moreover, the second World War has intensified
the degree of political as well as of economic co-operation
between the republics of the New World, politically, the
new-found solidarity of the western hemisphere rests upon
a delicate balance of forces. Between the United States and
the Latin American states there is little or no common
political tradition and no cultural unity. The civilizations
which the nations of the New World received from Europe,
like those which they have evolved, differ profoundly.

[1] See Humphreys, 'Latin America and the Post-War World', *Agenda*, ii
(Feb. 1943), pp. 84–9.

The distinction which is sometimes drawn between a materialistic civilization in the United States and the more spiritual values cherished in Latin America is, of course, intolerably crude. Nevertheless, the Latin American countries are deeply conscious of those elements, intellectual, psychological, and cultural, which divide them from what they are apt to regard as Protestant, Anglo-Saxon America. Until recent years it has been from the United States, not from Europe, that they have perceived the major threat to their way of life and to their political and economic independence; and, despite the 'Good Neighbour' policy, fear of the political and economic power of the United States is still deeply ingrained.[1]

These suspicions are greatest, at least they are most openly displayed, in Argentina. The Central American and island republics naturally revolve within the orbit of United States policy. With Mexico the political relations of the United States, studiously cordial, are in happy contrast to those which prevailed less than a quarter of a century ago. In South America, Brazil has made an *entente* with the United States almost a basic principle of its foreign policy. The susceptibilities of Argentina, however, have been reflected in an attitude of aloofness to the United States verging on hostility. Argentina is acutely aware of her own close economic ties with Europe. Her economy is competitive with, rather than complementary to, the United States economy. She has been deeply mortified by the exclusion of her meats from the United States market, ostensibly on the ground of their contamination with

[1] It is not lessened by such episodes as the philippic pronounced by Senator Hugh Butler in the United States Senate against certain aspects of United States policy in Latin America during the war. See *Expenditures and Commitments by the United States Government in or for Latin America* (78th Congress, 1st Session, Senate Document No. 132, Washington, Government Printing Office, 1943).

disease. Proud of her material prosperity, and for long confident of her superiority to the other Latin American states, she has resented United States influence in Latin America. She has aspired to something approaching hegemony at her end of the continent. She has taken the lead in opposition to the United States at successive Pan American conferences. Her record in failing to ratify Pan American conventions is unrivalled;[1] and between 1942 and 1945 Argentina ánd the United States became increasingly, even violently, estranged.

For all the Latin American states, however, and not only for Argentina, the United States is in the position of an over-mighty neighbour, and still, in many respects, a neighbour whose ways they find it difficult to understand. It has been the deliberate exercise of restraint by the United States, the mitigation of power by deliberate policy, that has made the growth of Pan Americanism possible. But the dangers of a clash between the rising nationalisms of the Latin American states and the United States are not therefore to be disregarded; and though it is probable that the United States will continue to show, in its Latin American policy, a studied regard for Latin American susceptibilities, the Latin American states, for their part, anxious, on the one hand, to preserve the regional safeguards established in the Pan American system, are likely, on the other, to continue to seek in Europe a counterbalance to the power and influence of the United States.

Only one European state, however, has ever occupied in relation to the independent Latin American states that special position which is now occupied by the United States. That state was Britain. In the nineteenth century Britain's

---

[1] For an excellent short account of Argentine–United States relations see C. H. Haring, *Argentina and the United States* (Boston, World Peace Foundation, 1941).

prestige in Latin America was unrivalled. Her financial and economic power was apparently inexhaustible. Her navy was the greatest in the world; and, just as the British Navy has always played a vital part in the defence of the Latin American states, so also Britain has contributed decisively to their economic development. The emancipation of Latin America initiated a century of Anglo-American rivalry over the trade and commerce of the new states. Between Britain and the United States there were, during the nineteenth century, occasional sharp conflicts over Latin American affairs; and there was even disagreement in principle. But though it was not till the end of the nineteenth century that Britain at length in large measure acceded to the interpretation of the Monroe Doctrine current in the United States, between British and United States policy there was always an essential conformity of outlook.[1] It was not, indeed, till the nineteen-thirties that this conformity was noticeably disturbed, and the divergence which then occurred between British and United States trading policy, in relation to certain of the Latin American countries, proved to be a potent source of misunderstanding, and gave rise to much resentment and suspicion in the United States.[2]

 The reasons for this divergency were, of course, to be found in the larger sphere of world economic policy and the consequences of the world depression; but it is clearly essential that there should be no such conflict of views or

---

[1] Cf. *ante*, pp. 48–50.

[2] Thus the Roca–Runciman Agreement of 1933 between Britain and Argentina and the subsequent agreement of 1936 were much resented in the United States. Britain has even been accused of deliberately encouraging Argentina in her aloofness to the United States and of tacitly supporting Argentine neutrality during the war. For a glaring example of irresponsible allegations, unsupported by evidence, see Ysabel Fisk and Robert A. Rennie, 'Argentina in Crisis', *Foreign Policy Reports*, xx (May 1944), p. 44.

clash of interests between Britain and the United States which might stimulate monopolistic tendencies, with political implications, or endanger the general harmony of Anglo-American relations. It is recognized that the expanding economies of the Latin American area cannot be solved within the framework of hemispheric self-sufficiency; it must equally be recognized that the general co-ordination of British and American with Latin American policies is vital to the interests and welfare of all parties concerned. British interests in Latin America are still important, widespread, and diversified, and a strong economic nexus exists between Britain and certain Latin American countries in particular. But it is not only to Britain that the Latin American area is linked; it is linked also to continental, and, particularly, to Latin Europe.

It is, of course, easy to exaggerate the importance of those traditional, intellectual, and sentimental ties which serve to bridge oceans and to link one civilization with another. In Latin America an educated *élite* has long been accustomed to look to Paris as the centre of the civilized world; but it is not more than an *élite*. Brazil and Portugal maintain a special and mutual regard; and, in Spanish America, the long aftermath of bitterness between Spain and her former colonies, which followed the revolutionary wars, and which was exacerbated by Spanish policy during the nineteenth century, has been at length succeeded by a revival of feeling for the mother country. But the movement known as *Hispanidad*, acceptable in many parts of Spanish America, in so far as it has meant a reaffirmation of a common measure of civilization, has been, in its intellectual manifestations, insufferably condescending, and, in its political aspects, singularly inept. Spanish America is more important to Spain than Spain to Spanish America; and the Spanish American states are as much

American (and many are in fact predominantly Indian and mestizo) as Spanish.

In each country, however, there are small groups, Catholic usually, and Conservative mainly, to whom these cultural, as well as commercial, connexions strongly appeal. It is, moreover, significant that Latin America has not been immune from the influence of contemporary European ideologies. German political influence accompanied the movement of German people and the rise of German trade, and the effect of National-Socialist doctrine, and of the German example, was clearly marked in military circles and among so-called 'nationalist' groups. Communist influence has been less obvious. Latin America has still no large industrial proletariat, and though Marxist theory has helped to mould some of the Latin American labour movements,[1] it is only in Chile and Cuba, and to a lesser extent in Mexico and Costa Rica, that a Communist party has flourished. Communism has not yet become a political force of the first order. The Communists, subject in most countries to varying degrees of repression, are still the whipping boys of politics; and, so violent is the fear that Communism has inspired, that it is only since 1942 that diplomatic relations have begun to be established between the Latin American states and Soviet Russia.[2]

But for Latin America, and for southern South America in particular, the attractive power of Europe is strong; in recent years the interplay of forces to which the Latin

---

[1] Sr. Lombardo Toledano, the leader of the Confederation of Latin American Workers, describes himself as a Marxist but not a Communist.

[2] They were maintained, however, between Mexico and the U.S.S.R. from 1924 to 1930, and between Uruguay and the U.S.S.R. from 1934 to 1935. On the general subject of Fascism and Communism, see Stephen Naft, 'Fascism and Communism in South America', *Foreign Policy Reports*, xiii (Dec. 1937), pp. 226–36, and J. C. Campbell, 'Political Extremes in South America', *Foreign Affairs*, xx (April 1942), pp. 517–34.

American area is exposed has been made sufficiently plain; and had Europe been successfully organized as an economic bloc on Nazi lines, it is doubtful, indeed, how long some of the Latin American states would, or could, have resisted its penetrative force. For all the American republics the Pan American system offers great advantages, and imposes corresponding obligations. It has evoked an increasing attachment, and, under favourable conditions, it is likely to grow stronger rather than weaker. But the war has in fact revealed its sources of weakness as well as its sources of strength, and though it may well operate, and with more powerful effect, within a wider system of political and economic security, it is not an alternative to such a system. The Act of Chapultepec is, and must be, complementary to the United Nations Charter.

The importance of Latin America to the rest of the world, moreover, and of the rest of the world to Latin America, is increasing, not diminishing; and the political and economic status of the Latin American countries, or at least of the major republics of South America, is itself changing. The Latin American states are no longer merely on the periphery of international relations. The time has passed when they could be treated simply as children at the international table, children whose part it was to be seen and not heard,[1] and not always, indeed, seen. Their role in international life is no longer merely passive; and some of them will expect, and may have the power, to play a far greater part in world affairs than heretofore.

This development is only of recent growth. At the first Hague Conference, in 1899, only one Latin American state, Mexico, was represented. All but two were present

---

[1] L. S. Rowe, C. H. Haring, S. Duggan, and D. G. Munro, *Latin America in World Affairs, 1914–1940* (Philadelphia, Univ. of Pennsylvania Press, 1941), p. 7.

at the second Hague Conference in 1907. But, before 1918, the Latin American countries hardly counted as world Powers; and it was the association of some of them in the first World War and the Paris Peace Conference, and the eventual participation of all of them in the League of Nations, that first brought to them a new international status.

Eight Latin American countries declared war on Germany in the war of 1914–18, though these, with the exception of Brazil, were not the largest or the most important,[1] and four severed relations with the Central Powers.[2] Eleven signed the Versailles Treaty, and ten, by ratifying the treaty, became original members of the League of Nations.[3] Six of the seven Latin American neutrals also became original members by accepting the invitation to accede to the Covenant within two months of its coming into force.[4] The majority of the Latin American states were thus members of the League before the first Assembly met

[1] Brazil, Cuba, Costa Rica, Guatemala, Haiti, Honduras, Nicaragua, Panamá. The Government of Costa Rica, which had come into power by force, was not recognized by the Allies, and Costa Rica was in the curious position of being at war with the only state that had recognized the then régime—Germany. The status of the Dominican Republic was also anomalous. From 1916 to 1924 the country was under United States military rule. After the entry of the United States into the war it cancelled the exequaturs of German consuls, but at that time it maintained no diplomatic relations with Germany; and it was a moot point whether the republic could be said to have severed relations or not. Neither country was invited to the Paris Peace Conference.

[2] Bolivia, Ecuador, Peru, Uruguay. For the role of the Latin American states in the war see P. A. Martin, *Latin America and the War* (Baltimore, Johns Hopkins Press, 1925).

[3] Ecuador neglected to ratify, and its entry into the League was delayed until 1934.

[4] Mexico was not invited, partly because its attitude to the war had been equivocal, partly because its Government was not recognized by the majority of the states present at the Peace Conference. Greatly offended, Mexico refused to apply for admission and only joined the League in 1931 on the express invitation of the Assembly.

in 1920, and all ultimately joined;[1] and the League not only appealed to Latin American idealism, as well as to considerations of security and prestige, at a time when feeling towards the United States was becoming increasingly embittered in Latin America;[2] it afforded a platform on which the Latin American states could make their voices heard in world affairs.

Some of these states, no doubt, joined the League with special ends in view; the degree of enthusiasm varied; and some ceased to participate when their special demands failed to win approval.[3] Argentina absented herself after the opening session, when her proposals for amending the Covenant were not accepted. This episode had been generally interpreted as due less to devotion to the principles of international organization than to jealousy of the position of Brazil at Geneva; and Argentina did not resume participation in the League until after Brazil, in 1926, offended by her failure to obtain a permanent seat on the Council, had herself withdrawn. In the thirties, moreover, withdrawals became numerous. Membership now was more a liability than an asset; the chief questions which occupied the League were not questions in which the Latin American states were intimately concerned; and as the authority of the League declined, so did Latin American interest in it.

But, from first to last, Latin American membership of the League was an important fact.[4] Uruguay, Colombia, and

[1] Costa Rica was granted admission in 1920 and the Dominican Republic in 1924.   [2] *Ante*, pp. 149–50.

[3] Thus Peru ceased to be represented between 1921 and 1929 and Bolivia between 1922 and 1929. Both states were offended because the League declined to review their long-standing territorial dispute with Chile.

[4] For the relations of the Latin American states with the League see W. H. Kelchner, *Latin American Relations with the League of Nations* (Boston, World Peace Foundation, 1930), M. Pérez-Guerrero, *Les Relations des États de l'Amérique Latine avec la Société des Nations* (Paris, Pedone, 1936), J. C. de

Cuba were consistently loyal, the Central American states, except Panamá, as consistently indifferent. But, after 1926, the Latin American states always had three seats on the Council. They possessed the means both of forwarding and of hindering the League's work; and on more than one occasion the action of the Latin American members, for good or ill, was decisive. In Latin America itself the political action of the League was always gravely embarrassed by the absence of the most powerful member of the Pan American Union—the United States—from Geneva, and co-operation between the Pan American Union and the League was far from close. But with the whole-hearted support of the United States the League was responsible, in 1933–4, for the peaceful settlement of the Leticia dispute between Colombia and Peru; and the work of the technical organs of the League met, in Latin America, with a considerable degree of success. Just as the Permanent Court of International Justice excited the perennial interest of the Latin American states, so also did the Committee on Intellectual Co-operation. The Latin American countries displayed, moreover, an increasing appreciation of the activities of the International Labour Office, which held, in 1936, its first regional conference of American members; and its expert advice on labour and social problems has been sought by more than one Latin American state.

At Geneva the Latin American states showed a considerable sense of solidarity, at least so far as their own interests were concerned, and the League both stimulated their self-reliance and enhanced their political importance But the presence and action of the Latin American states at

Macedo Soares, *Brazil and the League of Nations* (Paris, Pedone, 1928), and J. F. Rippy, *Latin America in World Politics* (New York, Crofts, 1938), pp. 267–75.

Geneva were not the only signs of their changing international status. There were further signs in the changed character of the Latin American policy of the United States in the nineteen-thirties, and there were signs also in the changing structure of Latin American economic life.

Economically, the relation of the Latin American countries to the rest of the world has been that of debtor to creditor, of miner, rancher, and farmer to manufacturer. Latin America, in the first century of its independent life, was the perfect example of what it is now fashionable to term a 'colonial' area. Its prosperity was dependent on the exchange of raw materials for manufactured products. Exports were its life-blood, and, from the point of view of the rest of the world, all the Latin American countries were, first and foremost, producers of foodstuffs and raw materials for export. While the United States normally exports less than a tenth of its national production, the Latin American countries export from one-third to one-half, and even higher proportions.[1] Each, moreover, specialized in one or two staple products, mineral or pastoral. In terms of value, minerals and their derivatives account for more than three-quarters of the exports of Chile, three-quarters of those of Mexico, and two-thirds of those of Peru. Bolivia is dependent on tin, Venezuela on oil, Colombia on coffee and petroleum. Cuba is the world's greatest exporter of cane-sugar. The Central American countries mainly depend on bananas and coffee. Brazil, though its economy is now more diversified, has turned from sugar to cotton and from rubber to coffee. Argentina

[1] Mordecai Ezekiel, 'Economic Relations between the Americas', *International Conciliation* (Feb. 1941), pp. 104, 108. In 1937 Latin America accounted for more than three-quarters of the world's exports of coffee, nearly three-quarters of its maize, nearly a half of its sugar, and more than a quarter of its wheat and copper. H. J. Trueblood, 'Raw Material Resources of Latin America', *Foreign Policy Reports*, xv (Aug. 1939), p. 115.

and Uruguay export the products of the farm and the ranch, and Argentina is not only one of the world's great granaries but its largest exporter of beef.

In the development of these natural resources foreign capital played much the same part as it played in the development of the Mississippi Valley in the United States. British and later United States capital, as well as Dutch, French, German, and Belgian, built the railways and the ports, operated the mines, developed the public utilities, the plantations and the oil-fields, and established the banks and the insurance companies. As early as 1825 more than £20,000,000 sterling had been invested by British subjects in Latin America.[1] By 1914 this sum had grown to nearly £1,000,000,000, and it had increased by another £200,000,000 by 1930. United States investments, starting late, and, till the first World War, lagging far behind, had by 1930 achieved a position of rough equality with British.[2]

There were, however, important differences in the role of foreign capital in the development of the United States and of Latin America. In the United States domestic capital itself accumulated and sought outlets at home and abroad; in the management of foreign enterprises in the United States American citizens took a controlling part; and the effects of capital investments promoted rather than discouraged industrialization. In Latin America, on the

---

[1] *Ante*, p. 46.

[2] British investments are greatest in Argentina, and a large part of all British investments in Latin America are in railway securities and government bonds. They are notoriously unremunerative. British figures are published regularly in the *South American Journal*. United States investments are largest in Cuba. For their size and distribution see R. L. Sammons and Milton Abelson, *American Direct Investments in Foreign Countries—1940* (U.S. Department of Commerce, Bureau of Foreign and Domestic Commerce, Washington, Government Printing Office, 1942). See also Soule, Efron, and Ness, *Latin America in the Future World*, p. 121.

other hand, the supply of native capital (traditionally invested in land) was always short; technical training and managerial experience were deficient; and foreign capital investments, rarely associated with domestic capital, had the effect of increasing rather than reducing the dependence of the Latin American countries for their trade and revenue on a few primary and staple commodities. The low purchasing power of the Latin American peoples, their relatively small populations, the shortage of skilled labour, local insufficiencies of two basic raw materials, coal and iron, and the dominant part played by the *hacienda* and the plantation system in Latin American society, similarly hindered the diversification of the Latin American economies.

Since 1914, however, this situation has been subjected to a radical change. The economies of the Latin American countries are still primarily agricultural and extractive economies. Latin American prosperity is still peculiarly dependent on the volume of world trade and the fluctuations of world prices. Nevertheless, in the period between the two wars, there has been a persistent attempt to reduce this dependence, to diversify the basis of Latin American economic life, and to achieve a more balanced and so more stable economic structure. This movement is associated with a spirit of economic nationalism, which is as much political as economic in inspiration, and which has for its end the achievement of what is commonly, though not altogether accurately, described as 'economic independence' of foreign Powers and foreign capital, or, in other words, the freeing of the elements of production and trade from external financial control. This has been in turn reflected in persistent attacks on the foreign-controlled insurance, extractive, and public utility enterprises.

These tendencies were first stimulated by the war of

1914–18, which suddenly revealed the dangers of too great a dependence on overseas markets and sources of supply. They were stimulated still further by the advent of the depression of the thirties; and the effects of the Great Depression, unlike those of the first World War, were far-reaching and permanent. The prices of the principal Latin American exports fell, by 1933, to little more than a third of their 1929 value.[1] The flow of capital to Latin America ceased, while rising tariff barriers and autarkic policies in the world at large forced the Latin American countries into an attempt to satisfy a larger proportion of their own needs. Government policy was now increasingly directed towards the development of domestic industries and the widening of the basis of primary production. Tariff barriers were raised, exchange controls imposed,[2] and a wave of nationalistic and restrictive legislation swept the Latin American countries. Even labour legislation was used as an instrument against the dominance of foreign capital, and the expropriations of the foreign-owned oil companies in Bolivia and Mexico were only the most spectacular examples of the new spirit of economic nationalism.

Meanwhile, the Latin American countries turned to industrialization with the manufacture of consumption goods; and what began as a movement of national defence became a permanent economic aspiration. In general the Latin American countries have learnt to provide themselves with a large part of the articles of common consumption. Argentina, Brazil (which exports textiles to Argentina), Mexico, and Chile are now the major manufacturing

[1] For the price collapse see Feuerlein and Hannan, *Dollars in Latin America*, pp. 19–21.
[2] See H. M. Bratter, 'Foreign Exchange Control in Latin America', *Foreign Policy Reports*, xiv (Feb. 1939), pp. 274–88.

states;[1] and it is significant that attempts are now being made to establish heavy industries in Brazil and Peru, as well as in Mexico.[2] The second World War, indeed, with the expansion of Latin American productive activities, and the curtailment of normal sources of supply, has given a fresh and decisive stimulus both to industrial development and to agricultural diversification,[3] and both of these movements have received the powerful support of the United States.

Not all the Latin American countries have yet attempted to break down a colonial economy; and industrialization is yet in its infancy. Its prospects are not uniformly encouraging, and it is subject to great limitations, from the point of view both of material and human resources. Though Latin America is one of the richest raw-material producing areas in the world, its people are poor, and the bulk of them are still engaged in subsistence farming. It is still in urgent need of capital and technical resources. Its labour supply is inadequate, its internal markets are still small, and the means of transportation are costly. The Latin American nations will long require the constructive aid which a genuinely co-operative system of international relations can afford them, though their needs may clash with their aspirations. But the economic structure of Latin America, and with it the pattern of its foreign trade, are visibly changing. Should industrialization lead, as many expect it to lead, to a rising standard of living and increased purchasing power, it will expand, not contract, the markets of Latin America, though it is bound to alter their character. Should its growth be even remotely comparable

[1] See *ante*, pp. 103, 114.

[2] The Volta Redonda iron and steel plant in Brazil, the Chimbote plant in Peru, and a similar plant at Monclova, Mexico.

[3] Involving, for example, the development of products such as rubber, fibres, vegetable oils, and drugs, formerly obtained from the Far East.

to that experienced in the United States between 1860 and 1910, the effect on the balance of world affairs would be similar to that caused by the emergence of the United States as a world Power at the beginning of the century. Even should it not, the political and economic power of the more important Latin American states has been much enhanced; their co-operation in world economic policy is essential; and in political affairs their views will increasingly have to be taken into account.

The War of 1939 to 1945, indeed, has brought to the Latin American states new opportunities and new responsibilities. All ultimately became belligerents,[1] and when, in 1944, a Brazilian expeditionary force was sent to Italy, for the first time in history an army from the New World, other than Canadian or American, fought overseas. But just as the war has revealed, not the independence of the New World, but its interdependence, political, economic, and strategic, with the Old, so the major problems of economic readjustment and political rehabilitation which the Latin American states face in the future can only be solved within the framework of a world order. The road before them is a difficult road. The perils revealed in their past experience still exist in the present. But if they can assume the responsibilities of their opportunities, the opportunities are theirs; and, for the rest of the world, what happens in Latin America is no longer to be lightly regarded.

---

[1] The six Central American and the three island republics entered the war in December 1941. Mexico declared war in May, and Brazil in August 1942. Bolivia became belligerent in April, and Colombia in November 1943. Chile, Peru, Ecuador, Paraguay, Venezuela, and Uruguay declared war on one or both remaining members of the Axis in February 1945, and Argentina's declaration of war took place in March.

NOTE ON SOURCES OF INFORMATION

The literature on Latin America is enormous. The references in the footnotes to this book are intended to supply the reader with a preliminary guide, but it would be both pedantic and misleading to repeat them here in the guise of a formal bibliography. Full bibliographical details have been given in the notes for each book or article on the first occasion that it has been cited. Here it is only necessary to indicate first the more general bibliographies to which the student must turn in order to discover what has been written on any particular aspect of Latin American history, and secondly the more obvious and accessible sources for the study of contemporary Latin American affairs.

(i) In the second edition of *A Bibliography of Latin American Bibliographies* (Library of Congress, Hispanic Foundation, Washington, Government Printing Office, 1942) Mr. C. K. Jones lists more than 3,000 items. His book is the starting-point for the research worker. For the general reader my own small selective and classified list of books, *Latin America* (Chatham House Bibliographies, published for the Royal Institute of International Affairs by the Oxford University Press, 1941), provides, I hope, a guide to the more authoritative material in English.

Much of the best work on Latin America, however, is not written in English, nor does it necessarily appear in the form of books. Besides Mr. Jones's work, cited above, therefore, the historical student should begin with three other outstanding general compilations. These are B. Sánchez Alonso, *Fuentes de la Historia Española e Hispano Americana* (2nd edn., 2 vols., Madrid, Centro de Estudios Históricos, 1927); *The Economic Literature of Latin America: a tentative bibliography*, compiled by the staff of the Bureau for Economic Research in Latin America (2 vols., Harvard Univ. Press, 1935–6); and S. F. Bemis and G. G. Griffin, *Guide to the Diplomatic History of the United States, 1775–1921* (Library of Congress, Washington,

Government Printing Office, 1935), which is in part a guide
to the diplomatic history of Latin America as well as to that
of the United States.

To the energy of American scholarship, moreover, which
puts our own unbibliographically minded nation to shame, we
are indebted for the invaluable annual *Handbook of Latin
American Studies* (edited by Lewis Hanke, 1936–40, and by
Miron Burgin, 1941– , Harvard Univ. Press, 1936–).
Beginning with the year 1935, this provides for writings on
Latin America an even more comprehensive guide than that
provided for the United States by the *Writings on American
History* (annual volumes, beginning with 1906, and published
from the volume for 1918 onwards by the American Historical
Association; edited by G. G. Griffin, Washington, Govern-
ment Printing Office, 1908–). Numerous periodicals,
American and Latin American, also record work in progress,
and, of these, two should be particularly noted: the *Hispanic
American Historical Review* (Baltimore, 1918–22; Durham, North
Carolina, 1926–), which is, to the student of Latin American
history, what the *American Historical Review* is to the student of
United States history, and the admirable *Revista de Historia de
América*, published by the Instituto Panamericano de Geografía
e Historia (Mexico, D.F., 1938–).

(ii) For the study of contemporary Latin American affairs
the debt to United States enterprise is again heavy. Since 1941
Professor A. P. Whitaker has edited the annual volume, *Inter-
American Affairs* (Columbia Univ. Press, 1942–), which is
accompanied by tables and maps. The *Inter-American Quarterly*,
originally the *Quarterly Journal of Inter-American Relations* (Cambridge, Mass., 1939; Washington, D.C., 1940–1), was all too
short-lived. It has been succeeded by the more popular but
useful *Inter-American Monthly*, now *The Inter-American* (Washington, 1942–), which provides, month by month, a variety of
information on contemporary developments in Latin America.
Valuable articles appear from time to time in *Foreign Affairs*, the
quarterly journal of the Council on Foreign Relations, New
York, in the fortnightly *Foreign Policy Reports* of the Foreign

Policy Association, New York, and in *International Conciliation*, published monthly by the Carnegie Endowment for International Peace. The monthly *Bulletin* and the numerous other publications of the Pan American Union (Washington, D.C.) vary in quality. Some, however, are highly informative. So also is the *Foreign Commerce Weekly*, published by the United States Department of Commerce. The *Inter-American Statistical Yearbook* (New York, Macmillan), which first appeared in 1940, and the late Professor P. A. Martin's *Who's Who in Latin America* (2nd edn., Stanford Univ. Press, 1940) are both useful works of reference.

In Latin America, apart from the growing volume of publications by the several governments, and such admirable reviews as the *Revista de Economía Argentina* (Buenos Aires, 1918–), the most important source is the Latin American press itself. *La Prensa* and *La Nación* of Buenos Aires, the former founded in 1869, and the latter in 1870 by Bartolomé Mitre, are more than purely Argentine newspapers. They gather news from all over the continent and their reputation is similar to that of the *New York Times* in the United States. They deservedly rank among the most distinguished newspapers in the world. Of other dailies it is perhaps sufficient to mention the *Estado de São Paulo* and the *Jornal do Commercio* of Brazil, *El Mercurio* of Chile, *El Tiempo* of Colombia, *Excelsior* of Mexico, and *La Mañana* of Uruguay.

Finally, those who are unable to see Latin America for themselves cannot do better than examine the photographs in the admirable collection made by J. L. Rich, *The Face of South America* (New York, American Geographical Society, 1942), the maps and charts in W. A. M. Burden, *The Struggle for Airways in Latin America* (New York, Council on Foreign Relations, 1943), and the remarkable series of maps, of South America, Peru, Chile, Mexico, Venezuela, and Brazil, published in *Fortune* (Jersey City) from December 1937 to June 1939.

Area and Population of the Latin American Countries

Country	Area in square miles	Population Last Census		Population Estimated	
Argentina	1,079,965	1914	7,995,000	1943	13,907,000
Bolivia	416,040	1900	1,816,000	1942	3,534,000
Brazil	3,286,170	1940	41,357,000		...
Chile	286,396	1940	5,014,000		...
Colombia	439,825	1938	8,702,000	1943	9,690,000
Costa Rica	19,238	1927	472,000	1942	687,000
Cuba	44,218	1931	3,962,000	1943	4,625,000
Dominican Republic	19,332	1935	1,479,000	1943	1,970,000
Ecuador	104,500 (estimate)	None complete		1942	3,086,000
El Salvador	13,176	1930	1,434,000	1943	1,880,000
Guatemala	42,364	1940	3,283,000		...
Haiti	10,700	None complete		1943	2,719,000
Honduras	59,161	1940	1,108,000		...
Mexico	758,258	1940	19,454,000		...
Nicaragua	53,668	1940	899,000		...
Panamá	28,575	1940	632,000		...
Paraguay	150,500	None complete		1941	1,040,000
Peru	513,924	1940	7,023,000		...
Uruguay	72,172	1908	1,043,000	1941	2,186,000
Venezuela	352,143	1941	3,468,000		...

INDEX

The names of authors and editors are entered in italics and the number following refers to the first occasion on which a work is cited. Footnotes are referred to by the letter 'f'.